M

PRAISE FOR

Therapy Demystified

"This book is a very welcome add........ ....
highly readable, clear but not overly simplified style, Kate S
her experience as a psychotherapist, a patient, and a motł
people find their way through the mental health maze: v
seek therapy, how to find a good therapist, how therapy woɪ
use it, and how to afford it. Especially helpful are Scharff's
of insightful questions and pointers (e.g., what to ask in the fiɪ
what are the signs of a bad therapist, how do you know you'ɪ

—Michael Stadter, PhD, Clinical Psychologist-in-Residence,
Dept. of Psychology, American University Faculty,
International Psychotherapy Institute Faculty,
Washington School of Psychiatry

"Anyone even considering g....... .... aɪout a
friend or loved one who may need tɪ ...... ɪng trained as a therapist in any mental health discipline wɪ. ...ɪ *Therapy Demystified* to be
an invaluable resource. In a time in which the mental health field can be
confusing, intimidating, and discouraging, Ms. Scharff has written a
book that is easy to understand, enjoyable to read, and filled with common sense. It offers a balanced overview of virtually the entire field."

—Michael H. Silver, PhD, MD, Assistant Clinical Professor,
Department of Psychiatry and Behavioral Sciences,
The George Washington University

"Kate Scharff's excellent (and reassuring!) book offers much for the
psychotherapy consumer. Whether you are seeking therapy for the
first time, have had bad therapy experiences in the past, or just want
assistance in finding effective and affordable help, this book is an
invaluable resource."

—Jane Prelinger, MSW, LICSW, Clinical Director,
Eugene Meyer III Treatment Center,
Washington School of Psychiatry
Faculty, Washington School of Psychiatry

DEC 0 2 2004

"Many readers will profit from Kate Scharff's book, *Therapy Demystified*. An experienced social worker, Scharff provides an 'insider's guide.' She has abundant practical suggestions: when to consider psychotherapy, how to find a good match in a therapist, what to expect from treatment, and even how to end it. She writes clearly and convincingly about different approaches to treatment. She's open about her preference for 'psychodynamic' therapy, asserting that the 'feelings–oriented' approach is essential. Dealing directly with insurance and with financial issues, Scharff notes that many patients earn more money as a result of their life progress in therapy. For the cash-strapped, she notes that high-quality treatment is available at low cost, through training institutes in many cities. Chapters about the special needs and issues of children, and about the who and where of community resources, provide more useful information.

"Scharff's book is a pleasure to read: straightforward, warm, and good-humored. She is upbeat but not simplistic, assertive but not prejudiced. The qualities she advocates in a good psychotherapist shine forth in her own prose."

—Brian B. Doyle, MD, Clinical Professor of Psychiatry
and of Family and Community Medicine,
Georgetown University School of Medicine, Washington, DC
Distinguished Life Fellow, American Psychiatric Association

KATE SCHARFF, MSW, is a licensed clinical social worker who has been practicing psychotherapy for fifteen years. She is the founder and director of Washington Services for Relationships in Transition, which offers clinical services to families going through high-conflict divorces. She is also co-chair of the Washington, D.C., satellite of the International Psychotherapy Institute, and runs a private therapy practice for individuals, couples, and families. She lives in Bethesda, Maryland.

THE COMPLETE DEMYSTIFIED SERIES

Insulin Pump Therapy Demystified
by Gabrielle Kaplan-Mayer

Bipolar Disorder Demystified
by Lana Castle

Borderline Personality Disorder Demystified
by Robert O. Friedel, MD

Therapy

Demystified

Therapy
Demystified

AN INSIDER'S GUIDE TO
GETTING THE RIGHT HELP
(WITHOUT GOING BROKE)

Kate Scharff, MSW

MARLOWE & COMPANY ■ NEW YORK

THERAPY DEMYSTIFIED:
An Insider's Guide to Getting the Right Help (Without Going Broke)
Copyright © 2004 by Kate Scharff, MSW

Published by
Marlowe & Company
An Imprint of Avalon Publishing Group, Incorporated
245 West 17th Street • 11th floor
New York, NY 10011-5300

AVALON
publishing group incorporated

Grateful acknowledgment is made to the following for permission to reprint
previously published material: American Psychological Association, for the
excerpt on pages 128–132, "Principles for the Provision of Mental Health and
Substance Abuse Treatment Services: A Bill of Rights" (copyright © 1997)

Library of Congress Cataloging-in-Publication Data
Scharff, Kate.
  Therapy demystified : an insider's guide to getting the right help—
without going broke / by Kate Scharff.
      p. cm.
  Includes bibliographical references and index.
  ISBN 1-56924-423-5 (pbk.)
  1. Psychotherapy—Popular works. I. Title.
  RC480.515.S337 2004
  616.89'14—dc22
                              2004015289

9 8 7 6 5 4 3 2 1

Designed by Pauline Neuwirth, Neuwirth and Associates, Inc.

Printed in the United States of America

For Chloe and Ben
And for Nell

∞

CONTENTS

INTRODUCTION

THE FACT THAT you're reading this book means you're considering therapy, either for yourself or for someone you love. You are far from alone; over twelve million Americans start therapy every year. And that's just the ones who go. Sadly, many who could be helped stay away due to misperceptions, doubts, fears, and questions that seem unanswerable. If you're thinking about therapy you're already feeling stressed and vulnerable. The last thing you need is to wade through a swamp of hard-to-find and hard-to-understand information about all the therapists out there. If you've ever wondered if therapy might help but felt skeptical, confused about the many types, lost as to where to begin, or afraid that you couldn't afford it, read on.

We're a nation of savvy shoppers. If we need a new CD player, we're likely to ask friends what they've bought, or consult *Consumer Reports* or online sites that review audio equipment. We might even visit more than one store. In the end, if we make a purchase we're not pleased with, or if the equipment doesn't work, we feel fine about returning it for another model. But when it comes to issues of our own happiness, we're uneducated consumers. Even most people in treatment know very little about the background or training of their therapists.

Why is that a problem? Try this analogy: let's say you suspect you've had a heart attack. You're scared and in pain. Your internist sends you to a specialist but gives you no information about her background or training. When you get to the new office, there are no framed diplomas affirming that you'll be seeing someone qualified to evaluate and treat your symptoms. To make matters worse, you don't even see posters with diagrams of the heart, information pamphlets about the practice, a receptionist, a nurse, or other patients in the waiting room. You begin to worry that you won't be seeing a cardiologist at all. For all you know, she could be a doctor of theology. This scenario isn't a reassuring start to a trusting professional relationship, but it's exactly how in-the-dark most people are when they first go to a therapist. And lack of information can actually be dangerous. Did you know that in this country it's legal for anyone, trained or not, to hang out a shingle and call himself a therapist?

I was born into a family of therapists, and I can't remember a time when I wasn't familiar with the culture and terminology of the mental health field. Not surprisingly, I'm a therapist myself. But recently I realized I had never really felt comfortable talking about my profession with people who weren't in the field. Here's what happened: My young daughter had a play date and I overheard the two girls chatting. My daughter asked her friend about her parents' jobs. Her friend answered that her mother was a doctor and her father was a teacher. As I listened, I felt a familiar tightening in my gut. I love my work, yet I found myself wishing—not for the first time—that it wasn't so hard to *explain*. But my kid didn't miss a beat: "My daddy works with computers and my mommy helps people with their problems and things they're worried about by talking about them," she offered.

"Cool," came the reply.

Hearing that simple exchange brought into focus for me the fact that as a group we therapists have done an abysmal job of demystifying what we do in a clear, direct fashion. If we were selling any other product, we'd have fired our marketing department a long time ago. Maybe because we're dealing in human emotions it feels crass to get practical. But that's backward, isn't it? It's precisely because our stock in trade is so precious that we should be much more candid about what we do.

The fact that we haven't done more to educate people about our work reinforces its stigma. While other fields have spokespeople who make their expertise clear and accessible to the general public, we've pretty much left our public relations to the media. The millions of people who gobble up Dr. Phil's pop psychology books every year or tune in to Dr. Laura have a deeper need than simply to satisfy their voyeurism. They need answers to the questions we all ask, such as "Why can't I be happy?" "Why can't I find someone to love me?" "Why am I so fearful?" or "Why do I keep repeating the same stupid behaviors?" But Drs. Phil and Laura do our profession a disservice by portraying it in a distorted way. While it's fun to watch a TV "shrink" bully a philandering husband into a contrite heap at the feet of his long-suffering wife—it's theater, not therapy. A media therapist is like a glistening, perfect piece of cheesecake in a television commercial. It looks tempting and delicious, but it's really Styrofoam and shaving cream—no nutritional value whatsoever.

Television and radio producers know how to trade on the universal longing for a magic bullet—some brilliant piece of advice that will solve everything. Successful media therapists are smart, articulate, charismatic performers, who can assess a complicated situation quickly and come up with a tidy formula to fix it. They're experts at zeroing in on their "client's" weak point, confronting him with it, and instructing him how to change. The problem is, they can't give him the means to do it. And since they're not trying to build an ongoing relationship, they don't even have to be tactful.

> **Television and radio producers know how to trade on the universal longing for a magic bullet—some brilliant piece of advice that will solve everything. Successful media therapists are smart, articulate, charismatic performers, who can assess a complicated situation quickly and come up with a tidy formula to fix it.**

For example, consider the philandering husband I mentioned. Let's say he's been cheating on his wife for years. She's finally had it, and drags him onto a television advice show. The host/expert, Dr. X, points out that the husband is cheating because he's mad at his wife for putting too much pressure on him to provide financially. Dr. X pronounces her critical, nagging, and sexually withholding, and her husband overworked, overwhelmed, and underappreciated. He suggests that the wife stop haranguing her husband and start accepting him for the good man and provider he is, and that the husband grow up, get a life, stop cheating, and face his responsibilities. Then, to drive home how devastating their fighting has been for the family, Dr. X interviews their traumatized children. The couple feels awful; how could they not have seen the error of their ways? Finally, Dr. X suggests some techniques for improving communication, and tells the couple to schedule a sacred "date night" once per month. All the advice is good. The humbled and grateful pair tearfully embraces and vows to turn over a new leaf. But what you don't see is that by the time the show airs they've already reverted to the old behaviors that make them miserable.

> **There's a strong force in all of us that pressures us to keep doing things in the same old way, even if that way doesn't work very well. And the older an established pattern is, the harder it is to alter.**

In real life, it's frustratingly hard to alter old patterns. At one time or another, all of us have detected negative behaviors in ourselves that we wanted to change but couldn't. For example, say you're one of the millions of people who use food for comfort. At some point in your early life, this behavior must have made sense. You weren't getting the emotional nurturing you needed, and since you were a child and relatively helpless, you took solace where you could—in food. As an adult you're no longer helpless, but you still reach for food when what you really need is emotional support. Telling yourself this is self-destructive doesn't help you stop. In fact, scolding yourself leads to shame, which leads to the need for more comfort, which leads to more eating. There's a strong force in all of us that pressures us to keep doing things in the same old way, even if that way doesn't work very well. And the older an established pattern is, the harder it is to alter.

But isn't it important to understand the roots of our problems? Sure. The first step toward change is often placing our behaviors in their historical contexts. If you're the hypothetical overeater, for example, it might be helpful to understand how your use of food as a substitute for love connects to your lonely childhood. But, by itself, an intellectual understanding of the roots of your problem can't help you make long-term changes. Why? Because ideas, no matter how right or smart they are, are in your head. And your problems are in your heart.

> **By itself, an intellectual understanding of the roots of your problem can't help you make long-term changes. Why? Because ideas, no matter how right or smart they are, are in your head. And your problems are in your heart.**

New patients often arrive in my consulting room expecting me to have all the answers. They want me to deliver, brilliantly. Explain. Fix. And why not? I'm supposed to be the expert. Something's not working for them, and they've come to me to tell them how to make it better. But even if, like Dr. Phil, I could understand a particular patient's problems right away and come up with a pithy directive—so what? I've been doing therapy long enough that sometimes I am able to quickly formulate a beginning understanding of what makes someone tick. And I'm the sort of person who is never at a loss for an opinion, nor the words to express it. But my outspokenness can be a professional liability. I've found out the hard way that, by and large, people don't take my advice—no matter how eagerly they request it or how good it is. And when patients fail to take advice, they usually end up feeling worse about themselves. That's not therapeutic.

If you want to change your hairstyle, fine; you might accept advice from your stylist. But the tough truth is that if you want to change something inside yourself, such as a way you feel, think, or behave, you need more than someone pointing out your mistakes and telling you how to fix them. The only road to lasting, substantial change is facing your emotions and dealing with them in a new way. Real therapists are not gurus or mind readers. They're supporters, guides, and interpreters. And real therapy isn't prescriptive. It's a collaborative relationship, based on trust and nonjudgmental acceptance, in which you and a caring professional work together to understand you better.

> **The tough truth is that if you want to change something inside yourself, such as a way you feel, think, or behave, you need more than someone pointing out your mistakes and telling you how to fix them. The only road to lasting, substantial change is facing your emotions and dealing with them in a new way.**

Therapy has become such an integral part of our culture that we talk about it in shorthand, as if we all know what we mean. But we don't, not really. For too long most Americans have viewed therapy through a mysterious haze. On its most basic level, therapy is about bringing secrets into the light; about making the unknown known, and thereby less ominous. In this book I've tried to provide good answers, in plain English, to all your therapy questions, such as:

- Do I really need therapy?
- How does therapy actually work?
- What are the different kinds of therapists, and which would be best for me?
- Where can I find a therapist *I can afford?*
- What about all the bad things I've heard (or experienced!) about therapy?
- What will the first session, and subsequent ones, be like?
- How can I tell a good therapist from a bad one?

- How can I get the most out of my therapy?
- How can I tell if my child needs therapy, and what do I do if she does?
- What if my loved one needs therapy but won't go?
- How can I tell if I'm making progress?
- How do I know when I'm done?

Therapy done well, by the right professional, is an affordable, powerful aid for a broad range of people with a wide range of problems. No matter who you are, where you live, or the nature of your emotional struggles, there's good quality, affordable help available if you want it. I wrote this book to give you all the information you need to figure out when to seek therapy, where to find it, and how to make it work for you.

PART ONE

To Go or Not to Go?

ONE

When to Get Help

WE ALL EXPERIENCE emotional ups and downs. If you get divorced, you'll be hurt, angry, and scared. If someone close to you dies, you'll have to grieve. If you're having difficulties at work, you'll feel stressed and anxious. Obviously, it's not realistic to expect to be happy all the time. So how do you know when your problem is of the everyday sort that's likely to resolve on its own, and when it merits therapy?

Some people seek therapy because they suffer an emotional "symptom" that's serious enough that it interferes with daily life. Examples are persistent sadness, worries or fears, unresolved anger, and lack of sexual desire. Others go into therapy because they're experiencing conflict in their interpersonal relationships, such as prolonged or intense difficulties with a romantic partner or close friend, trouble making or keeping friends, or difficulties with authority. Another group wants help with problematic behaviors, such as eating disorders or addictions. Some people want help getting "unstuck," say from an unsatisfying career or an unhealthy relationship. Even those who don't have a problem per se but feel generally empty or unfulfilled sometimes go to therapy to improve the quality of their emotional lives.

Actually, there's probably a combination of factors prompting you to consider getting help. After all, a problem in one area of your life affects the other areas. If you're depressed, your marriage, work, and parenting suffer. If you're fighting with your spouse, you may become depressed and lose interest in work. The issues can get tangled and confusing. But you don't need a clear definition of what's bothering you before you seek therapy. As a matter of fact, having a predetermined notion of what's wrong can get in the way of being open to new ideas that might emerge after you start.

> **You don't need a clear definition of what's bothering you before you seek therapy. As a matter of fact, having a predetermined notion of what's wrong can get in the way of being open to new ideas that might emerge after you start.**

Think of it this way: Say you had a cough and a runny nose. These are pretty innocuous symptoms; you'd likely chalk them up to a common cold or allergies and live with them for a while. But what if these symptoms lingered for weeks, or if you developed a hacking cough and a fever? You'd have no way of knowing if you were suffering the normal course of a virus or if you had a treatable infection. So, you'd go to physician, who would either tell you to wait it out or give you an antibiotic. Just as you rely on a medical practitioner to tell you if your body needs medicine, you can rely on a mental health practitioner to tell you if you need therapy. When in doubt, get a consultation.

Probably the best clue that it's time to see a therapist is a sense that some way you're thinking, feeling, or behaving has been interfering with the normal living of your life, over a significant period of time. You're immobilized, overwhelmed, or out of your depth. The subjective experience of discomfort and the wish to do something about it are the only prerequisites for therapy.

Here is a list (not exhaustive, but a good start) of the kinds of problems that should prompt you to consider getting help:

- You feel isolated.
- You feel troubled by patterns in your personal or professional relationships.
- People suggest you should "get help."
- You suffer with an addiction (for example, to alcohol or other drugs, or to a problematic behavior, such as gambling or overeating).
- You suffer with a phobia (for example, you're afraid to ride elevators, fly, or leave your house).
- You're grieving a loss, but people tell you that you should be "over it" by now.
- You're having trouble adjusting to a medical diagnosis or dealing with the symptoms of medical illness.
- You have feelings of anxiety that are "free-floating" (not attached to any particular situation or event).
- You have a case of the blues that never goes away, or is present too much of the time.
- You feel angry most of the time.
- You feel tired, listless, or lethargic.
- You no longer take pleasure in activities that you used to enjoy.
- You have lost interest in sex.
- You feel helpless or hopeless.
- You suffer from the irrational fear that something terrible will happen to you or someone you care about.
- You have persistent or intrusive upsetting thoughts.
- You have been assaulted or abused.
- You feel chronically disappointed in yourself and/or other people.
- You find it hard to think clearly or make decisions.
- You sleep too much or too little.
- You eat too much or too little and have lost or gained a considerable amount of weight.
- You feel grumpy or irritable.

- You feel restless or agitated.
- You don't trust your sense of yourself.
- You don't trust your sense of reality.
- You are having trouble coping or adjusting to a circumstance in your life.
- You have had thoughts of hurting yourself.
- You have had thoughts of hurting others.
- You want to die.

Life is unpredictable. The best we can hope for is to be able to adapt to its vicissitudes and enjoy its pleasures in a way that feels honest to our natures. Our mental health can be measured in terms of our ability to face each new developmental task—whether it's adolescence, marriage, the birth of a child, or the loss of a parent—and emerge enriched from the experience. But at some point in our lives most of us will get emotionally overwhelmed. At that point we will not be free to be our best, most fulfilled, most creative selves. Therapy can help us get back on track.

> **At some point in our lives most of us will get emotionally overwhelmed. At that point we will not be free to be our best, most fulfilled, most creative selves.**

A Special Word on Suicidal Feelings

All of us, at one time or another, have considered our own deaths. When we reflect on the issue of suicide, though, it is generally as a concept, rather than a viable option. For most of us, thoughts of killing ourselves are fleeting, or a dramatic flourish masking our wish to know how important we are to people we love ("You'll be sorry when I'm gone!"). But for others, thoughts of death are very real symptoms of a serious depression. If you ever experience suicidal feelings, do not wait. Seek psychiatric help immediately, even if it means going to the emergency room of your local hospital. Don't worry that your feelings will be judged as "just a cry for help." All emotional pain is a cry for help, and all people in emotional pain should get the help they deserve. Similarly, if someone you know mentions suicidal feelings, even in passing, suggest that he get help immediately. If someone is actively suicidal, call the police. The wish to die is not a part of normal experience, and should always be taken seriously.

Are There Any Special Characteristics That Make Someone a Good Candidate for Therapy?

Perhaps you're worried you won't be good at being in therapy. A surprising number of people stay away because they think they're not smart or verbal enough to be good clients.* The truth is, a lot of people aren't adept at talking about their feelings—or even recognizing what those feelings are. If you're someone who finds it difficult or painful to talk about yourself, that's okay. A therapist's job is to help you make sense of your emotions, and to do it without embarrassing you by being confrontational or intrusive.

Psychological sophistication is not a prerequisite for therapy; you don't need any kind of special education to be good at it. As a matter of fact, understanding yourself too well can sometimes be a hindrance. Successful therapy is based on feeling, not thinking. Intellectual understanding alone doesn't lead to growth, and can sometimes be used to keep feelings at bay. If you're motivated, feel prepared to participate actively, and have chosen a therapist you like and feel confident in, you'll do fine.

> **Psychological sophistication is not a prerequisite for therapy; you don't need any kind of special education to be good at it.**

---

* Some therapists refer to the people they treat as "clients," while others prefer the term "patients." I've used the terms interchangeably in this book.

When an Adult You Love Needs Therapy

It's painful to watch a loved one suffering, whether it's a family member or a friend. But how you cope will depend on the nature of the relationship and the way his or her difficulties affect you.

Say a close friend becomes depressed. She withdraws from your social group and seems to spend most of her time on the Internet, watching television, or in bed. Her marriage is stressed as a result, and her teenage children are acting out in school. You become increasingly concerned, and you want to help. What to do?

By all means, you should tell her you're concerned and suggest she get help. You might even furnish her with a referral. Be specific about which behaviors you see that trouble you. Tell her you miss the time you used to spend together. But if your friend is resistant, don't offer to set up an appointment for her. Most therapists won't allow you to anyway, because they know therapy can't succeed unless it's initiated by the client (unless the client is a child).

It's hard to accept our powerlessness to change people we love, particularly if their suffering affects us directly. Take Jenny, for example, a client who came to see me because her husband, Dan, who suffered from depression, had lost interest in sex. Through her tears, she explained that six months earlier Dan had lost his job. At first, he had energetically pursued employment, but as the weeks slipped into months without success, his self-esteem plummeted. Not only had he withdrawn from intimacy with Jenny, but he had stopped showing much interest in their young children. Now Jenny, who had been forced to take work as a bookkeeper in order to keep the family out of bankruptcy, feared that Dan had stopped looking for work. When she begged him to get help, he became angry and defensive, accusing her of thinking that his unemployment was his fault. To make matters worse, Jenny could tell that his problems were taking a terrible toll on their children, who had begun to fight among themselves more than usual, and to bring home poor report cards.

Since Dan's problem was affecting the whole household and he was refusing treatment, I suggested family therapy. Jenny announced to her husband that she had scheduled a session, and was planning to bring the children. She said she hoped he would come along. Dan refused to come to our first appointments. But with help, Jenny was able to speak more directly with her children about their family situation and to give them the space they needed to voice their concerns and fears. With the support therapy provided, Jenny and the children were able to cope better with the stress of Dan's depression.

I encouraged Jenny not to pressure Dan to come, but to let him know he was missed. After a few sessions, Dan grudgingly joined us. When he heard his family speaking honestly, but not accusingly, about their concerns for him, he accepted a referral from me to see a colleague, a psychiatrist, who could evaluate his depression. Dan and the psychiatrist agreed to try an antidepressant medication and therapy. Within a few weeks, Dan's depression had lifted to the point that he was able to participate fully in the family therapy. He began to search for a job in earnest once more, and to spend his extra time helping out around the house and planning activities with his children. When he found a new job two months later, we mutually agreed to end the family work. Dan and Jenny continued with me as a couple to work on their sex life, in which Dan now had a renewed interest.

Dan was not initially motivated to change. If Jenny had dragged him in at the beginning of our work, the whole process might have failed. In general, haranguing someone you love to go "get fixed" doesn't work. You're much better off seeking treatment for yourself, both for help coping with the situation and to examine your own contribution to it. A family is an interconnected set of relationships. If one person changes, everyone feels it. Dan came to treatment when he saw his wife and children dealing directly with his depression and moving out of their helpless and guilty positions. Their emotional separation from his problem made him feel left behind, and that gave him a powerful reason to join the therapy. Once he did, and realized that his fears of being attacked and vilified were unfounded, he saw that his family still loved him and he began to participate.

Is Therapy Ever a Bad Idea?

While therapy is helpful for a wide range of problems, it's not for every person or every situation, such as when:

- ## *You're convinced the problem lies outside of you*

  Occasionally people come to therapy to complain. If you're sure that you're married to a louse, your boss is out to get you, you have chronically bad luck, and that all your unhappiness is completely out of your control, then therapy might not help. Using therapy as a series of gripe sessions might even distract you from taking the actions necessary to make your life better.

  On the other hand, it just may be that in therapy you'll find some better ways to cope with an unchangeable situation, or learn how you're making it worse than it has to be. Therapy is mostly about understanding your own role in things. So even if it turns out your husband *is* a louse, you'll have more options than you thought for dealing with him.

  > **It just may be that in therapy you'll find some better ways to cope with an unchangeable situation, or learn how you're making it worse than it has to be.**

- ## *You want your therapist to be an ally in changing someone else*

  Often people believe that their own wishes will carry more weight if they come out of the mouth of a therapist. As a couple therapist, I meet lots of disgruntled spouses who bring their partners to me hoping I'll knock some sense into them. The result is that the "difficult" spouse feels as if he's been dragged to the principal's office for a scolding. Casting your therapist in the role of disciplinarian or co-conspirator is a recipe for failure. You'd do better to ask yourself if there's a problem in your relationship that *you* can take responsibility for. Then get help to work on that. Once you do, your spouse may be more open to therapy.

What About "Mandated" Therapy?

Occasionally, someone will be required to get therapy as a result of a legal proceeding. For example, judges will often mandate therapy for families going through difficult divorces. When someone is forced into treatment, even if her need is great, the odds of success are nowhere as good as if she had come voluntarily. But even so, a surprising number of people get help despite their objections. As in the example of Dan and Jen, people who come to therapy reluctantly can sometimes develop hope and an openness to new ways of seeing and doing things. Even if you're in therapy because you have no choice, you might eventually get some real benefit.

Complements to Therapy

Therapy doesn't alleviate the environmental problems of living. If, for example, you're coping with a mentally or physically ill relative, a learning-disabled child, or an aging parent with dementia, you could probably benefit from the support of peers who have experience dealing with similar issues. If you struggle with an addiction, you'll almost certainly need the help of a group like Alcoholics Anonymous or Narcotics Anonymous. You will find many such self-help groups listed in the "Resources" section of this book.

Self-help programs and therapy aren't mutually exclusive, although sometimes the Twelve Step programs say they are. Self-help groups can be a good precursor to therapy, by helping identify the psychological aspects of a problem you need to work on more deeply. Self-help groups can also be a good adjunct to therapy, by offering you additional support and helping with the practical aspects of your problem.

TWO

The Top Ten Misguided Reasons for Avoiding Therapy

For SOME PEOPLE, getting emotional help is exciting, even fun. They look forward to the opportunity to talk about themselves and feel supported. But many others view the whole enterprise with skepticism and mistrust. Even though mental health treatments don't carry the heavy stigma they once did, I've run across many people who could clearly benefit from therapy but were dead set against the idea. I've met lots of others who suspected that therapy could be useful but were on the fence, staying away because of nagging worries of various kinds.

Not everyone needs help (see Chapter One). But it would be a shame if you could benefit from therapy but missed out simply because of outdated notions or misinformation. Over the years I've compiled a hit parade of the most popular unfounded concerns that keep people away from therapy. Maybe you'll recognize some of your own.

1. I can't afford it.

I put this one first because it's by far the most prevalent misconception. The truth is that even if you're on a tight budget, there's good therapy out there you can afford. I know that many people consider therapy a luxury, but I find this puzzling. With the exception of the basics—food, shelter, and physical health—there's nothing more important than the quality of your emotional life. What could be more valuable than your happiness? Luckily, you don't have to choose between your other financial responsibilities and therapy, because there are some really great bargains to be had. I will discuss them in detail in Chapter Seven.

> **You don't have to choose between your other financial responsibilities and therapy, because there are some really great bargains to be had.**

Here's something else to consider: studies show that an individual's income is very likely to increase as a result of psychotherapy. In fact, many people find they actually have more disposable income after they enter therapy than they did before.

I can attest to this from personal experience. When I was a graduate student in my early twenties, I could barely make ends meet. I badly needed therapy but couldn't imagine how I would pay for it. Finally, I bit the bullet and entered analysis (for an explanation of the difference between analysis and other forms of therapy, see Chapter Three). Even though I was given a significantly reduced rate, the fees amounted to almost half my meager income. I was panicked.

What I discovered was that even though I had to do without some extras to afford my therapy, I was able to do so without a lot of difficulty. As I was forced to become more thoughtful about my expenditures, I also came to grips with the fact that I had a lifelong problem of overspending and, as a result, depriving myself of things I really needed.

My situation was extreme; I'm definitely not suggesting you spend half your income on therapy. After all, at the time I went into analysis I was training to be a therapist myself, so it made extra sense to make my therapy a priority. But my experience illustrates the four reasons you might find therapy less of a financial strain than you fear:

- People in therapy feel supported emotionally and therefore less deprived than they did before. If you're someone who tends to overspend in an attempt to comfort yourself, you're less likely to do once you start.
- Therapy is not only a place to discuss purely emotional issues; it's also a place to discuss practical issues, such as budgeting.
- Therapy is a good place to explore obstacles to maximizing your own earning potential.
- The responsibility for the therapy fee, if it's not too burdensome, can encourage you to become more financially organized.

And remember, while therapy is not forever, its benefits to your money management and earning skills are yours to keep.

2.   I don't have time.

It may seem that you just can't shoehorn another appointment into your already crammed schedule. Before you send therapy to the bottom of The List of Things You'll Do for Yourself When Life Slows Down, let's think about this a bit more.

You may have already calculated that if you go into therapy once per week for fifty minutes, and you're lucky enough to find a therapist within, say, twenty minutes of your office or home, you'll have to budget ninety minutes each week for therapy. But maybe you have a demanding job with an inflexible boss who wouldn't look kindly on your slipping out for a long lunch. And where would you say you were going, anyway? Maybe you also have a family already lobbying for your scarce time. Perhaps, on top of it all, you're taking night classes or working a second part-time job to make ends meet. All of our lives are some version of this circus.

First, you should know that therapists are often quite sympathetic to the demands of a busy schedule. Many offer early morning and late evening appointments for people with inflexible work schedules, or have located their offices to be convenient for working people. Others have flexible cancellation policies, or will conduct sessions by telephone if something comes up at the last minute and you can't make it in.

Second, time is like money in the sense that, often, how much or little of it you have is a subjective experience rather than an objective amount. We all know someone who is impressively productive. Say it's a friend who works full-time at a challenging career, exercises, finds time for extracurricular activities and entertaining, and makes it to every PTA meeting, yet doesn't seem inordinately stressed. It's true that people have varying amounts of energy and tolerance for being on the go. Some people need a lot of downtime, and others don't. But it's also true that busy people are often organized people, and organized people get more done. Most of my patients find, as I did, that allocating time for therapy results in their having more disposable time then they used to. With time as with money, not having enough is usually a matter of how we spend it, and therapy helps us spend it more wisely.

Third, if you don't have ninety minutes a week to spare, even on something as important as your own happiness, then something is wrong. If you're genuinely overbooked, it could be you're taking on tasks that should be delegated to others. Perhaps the issue is one of time management, of ordering your priorities, or of difficulty saying "no" when people ask you to do things. Maybe you feel harried and stressed to the point where you're not taking pleasure in tasks you'd otherwise enjoy. All of these issues could be explored in therapy.

Fourth, therapy is a good time investment because it makes everything else you do easier. If you've been unhappy for even a few months, you may have lost your perspective on how mentally and physically draining it can be to feel that way. Our emotional conflicts, whether they're small (like pebbles in our shoes) or big (like anvils around our necks), distract, preoccupy, and exhaust us. It requires effort, sometimes tremendous effort, to battle on in the face of them. And that leaves less emotional energy left over for us to use in productive ways, such as paying attention to the people we love or advancing our careers. In fact, it takes a lot more energy to function *in spite* of our problems than it does to talk about them in therapy. Rather than finding therapy to be another onerous task that saps your energy, like picking up the dry cleaning or going to the dentist, you're likely to find that it mentally organizes and energizes you. Even if—*especially* if—the topics you discuss are painful, good therapy will leave you with more emotional zest for the other parts of your life.

> **If you've been unhappy for even a few months, you may have lost your perspective on how mentally and physically draining it can be to feel that way.**

3. Talking about my problems will only make them worse.

Many people tell me they stay away from therapy because they think they'll be asked to dredge up painful memories and feelings they'd just as soon not think about. Perhaps you feel this way, too. Maybe you're sure that whatever your current problems are, they're not as bad as the pain you'd feel if you had to talk about what happened to you years ago. In other words, "what you don't know can't hurt you." Actually, the opposite is true.

Think of your emotional energy as money in your psychic bank. You have a finite amount. Choosing *not* to think about or remember something doesn't come free—in fact it's very costly. Once you force, say, a painful memory out of your awareness, it's not really gone. It's just exiled to your unconscious (see Chapter Five), where it lurks and threatens to break back through. You will have to continue to spend emotional money in order to keep it there. This process of banishing an unwanted feeling, memory, idea, or wish from your conscious mind and keeping it in exile is called "repression." Repression is mentally expensive; doing it costs more emotional currency than facing your problems head-on.

> **Repression is mentally expensive; doing it costs more emotional currency than facing your problems head-on.**

Beyond draining us emotionally, past events, feelings, and relationships that we try not to think about have other influences on the ways we feel and behave now. As an example, let's consider Larry, the divorced father of a ten-year-old girl I see in therapy. I asked him to come see me because his daughter had been complaining that she was afraid of her weekend visits with him. She tearfully told me that he had a volatile temper. He was extremely critical of her and her younger sister, often becoming explosively angry at them for small misbehaviors. She described how, out of the blue, he frequently erupted with rage, yelling, threatening, and sometimes hitting them. Eventually, he would calm down and then, feeling remorseful and ashamed, would ask their forgiveness. My patient loved her father and wanted to be close to him, but felt understandably unsafe and mistrustful. She also felt guilty about her mistrust, since he clearly felt so bad about his angry outbursts.

When I saw Larry, he acknowledged his problem with managing frustration and anger, and said he often did lash out at his daughters in ways he felt very bad about. In fact, it had been his temper that had driven his wife away. Larry said that he had resolved many times to stop lashing out at his loved ones, but had never succeeded for long. When his children argued with each other or talked back rudely to him, or when someone disappointed him or let him down, he felt overwhelmed with rage.

Larry was reluctant to talk about himself. Eventually, he did tell me that his own parents had divorced when he was ten. His mother had abandoned the family, and he had been left to the care of his father, an alcoholic with a terrible, abusive temper, who beat his children. As Larry spoke about his father, his eyes filled with tears. I pointed out that this was a painful topic for him. He said it was, but that he tried not to think or talk about it. In fact, he had cut off all contact with his father, who lived only a few miles away.

Larry's reluctance to talk about his painful past was easy for me to understand. Nevertheless, I pointed out that there was a connection between his father's violent temper and Larry's own that would be worth exploring. Larry refused to discuss the matter further, saying he knew his own problems with anger management were connected to his past, but since he couldn't change the past he didn't want to dwell on it. He would just make more of an effort to control himself around his children.

A month later, Larry was back in my office, upset about another incident with his children. Over dinner, his two girls had squabbled, and one had spilled a glass of milk. Before he knew what he was doing, Larry had slapped her, hard, across the face. I said he must be feeling very ashamed, the same way he had felt when he had been hit by his own father. And the worst part was that he was behaving just like his father, in the way he most wanted not to. Even though Larry was frightened of the feelings he was going to have to face, he accepted a referral from me for a therapist of his own. Within weeks, my little patient reported improvements in her relationship with her father; the angry outbursts had stopped. When I spoke to Larry a few months into his therapy, he reported that he still felt sad about his father, but also tremendously relieved. He realized that what had been keeping him from talking about his past was mostly the shame he felt about it. "But after all," he said "I was only a little boy when he did those things to me. Now I am a man, and I can make my own decisions." These days, Larry is feeling much better about himself, and even considering initiating contact with his father. And his daughter is feeling much safer with him, too.

Larry's experience illustrates another critical point: therapists don't put ideas in people's heads, they just illuminate the ones that are already there. Think of your mind as a dark room, and your old worries and fears as the furniture you bump your shins on as you stumble around, unable to see. A therapist can turn on the light so you can navigate better.

> Therapists don't put ideas in people's heads, they just illuminate the ones that are already there. Think of your mind as a dark room, and your old worries and fears as the furniture you bump your shins on as you stumble around, unable to see. A therapist can turn on the light so you can navigate better.

4. People in therapy are whiny and self-indulgent.

Nobody likes a complainer. We all know people who wallow in their past misfortunes and blame their problems on others. People (like Larry in the above example) who come from the "pull yourself up by your bootstraps" school of life often have disdain for therapy because they think it encourages people to sit around feeling sorry for themselves.

Actually, the reverse is true. The point of therapy is to help you take responsibility for your life by dealing with the ideas, feelings, or conflicts that hold you back. If you get stuck in therapy going over and over the same emotional territory, your therapist should help you to get unstuck.

Consider Lisa, who came to me for therapy because she was unhappy in her marriage. For several months, in weekly sessions, she complained that her husband was lazy, self-involved, and unreliable. She didn't think it was entirely his fault; she was able to talk about her own contribution to their difficulties. But in the end every conversation circled back to the ways her husband had let her down, so the overall effect was to confirm that it was, after all, mostly him.

Initially, Lisa enjoyed therapy because she felt she had a place to vent her frustrations and feel supported. But after a few sessions she realized that using therapy as a place to vent wasn't helping her improve things. If anything, it was contributing to her staying stuck, since "getting the anger out" in sessions left her more able to tolerate the stifling sameness of her marriage.

One day, Lisa admitted to me that she worried about boring me with her constant railings against her husband. I acknowledged it *was* difficult to hear the same complaints week after week and to see her feeling hopeless. After all, we didn't have the power to change her husband. We explored the "stuckness" she felt: She was married to a man who disappointed her, but she loved him and wanted to stay with him. She couldn't fix him, yet she couldn't accept him the way he was.

Lisa had needed to complain in therapy for a while in order for me to understand, and for her to really experience, how helpless she felt. But after that, our work changed direction. The box she felt trapped in was in many ways her own construction. After all, she had chosen her husband, and she was choosing to stay with him now. In the safe setting of therapy, as she examined her self-perception as a martyr in her marriage and other areas of her life, Lisa began to remember the good qualities in her husband that had drawn her to him in the first place. Over time, she became less critical and, to her surprise and delight, her spouse responded by being more attentive. Things between them, while not perfect, began to improve.

5. Talking to a stranger won't help me— that's what my friends and family are for.

Friends and family, teachers, clergy, and professional mentors can and should be invaluable sources of support in our lives. But there are a number of reasons they can't help you the way a therapist can:

- Friends are not neutral. Even if they want the best for you, they have a personal investment. Whatever support or advice they offer will be biased according to their own agendas. And they aren't trained to factor these agendas out.
- You won't feel free to share everything with your friends.

After all, friends are people you see socially, and you are likely to hold some things back, even if you're not aware of doing so.

- Even a good friend may not be able to provide confidentiality.
- Good friendship is mutual give and take. In therapy, unlike in friendship, you won't be expected to spend equal time focusing on the therapist's problems and needs. The time will be only for you.
- Friends don't have the professional training and experience a therapist brings to bear in helping you.

6. I'll be in therapy forever.

Perhaps you're afraid if you start you'll be encouraged to stay for years. Maybe you're worried you'll be turned into a "lifer," or become dependent on your therapist. Or worse, if you don't like him, feel the therapy isn't working, or eventually get better and want to leave, your therapist will try to hold on to you.

If it goes well, your relationship with your therapist *will* be important. Especially in the beginning, you may find yourself wondering what she might think about something, or looking forward eagerly to your next session so you can tell her about something that's happened. Hopefully, you'll feel comforted and supported. But a good therapist doesn't strive to make himself indispensable or encourage you to hang on his every word. He'll help you understand yourself better and develop tools you can use in your own life to feel more fulfilled, get along better with people, and live and work more effectively. A good therapist is working toward being out of a job.

> **A good therapist is working toward being out of a job.**

Also, most therapy is brief. While some people can benefit from a longer stint, many get the help they need from just a few sessions (we'll discuss the indications for brief and long-term therapy in Chapter Nine).

7. Therapy is for crazy people.

A surprising number of people still think of therapy as a treatment reserved for the mentally ill. Actually, since it's a partnership requiring you to be a thoughtful and active participant, a fundamentally well-put-together person who functions in life but struggles in a few key areas will do better in therapy, have more types of treatment available to him, and improve more quickly than someone with a serious mental illness.

In our culture, many psychiatric terms have come into common parlance. We call someone "schizophrenic" if she changes her mind a lot, "anal" if he's overly neat, or "obsessive-compulsive" if she's bound by routine. If a boy is very close to his mother, we might say he has an Oedipus complex. We use these terms jokingly, but they have a nasty ring.

No one wants to be labeled, or summed up in clinical shorthand. If your idea of a therapist is someone emotionally detached and ready to spew technical jargon, then I'm not surprised you've stayed away. Every adequately trained therapist is required to have been in therapy herself—often intensely and for many years—and has respect for the courage and commitment required. Starting therapy is an act of hope, and therefore a sign of health.

> **If your idea of a therapist is someone emotionally detached and ready to spew technical jargon, then I'm not surprised you've stayed away.**

8. I just want to work on a specific problem; a therapist will dredge up my whole life.

In therapy, you're the boss. If you want to resolve a particular problem, a good therapist will respect that. Say, for example, you're in a committed relationship with someone who wants to get married, but you're ambivalent. It would be reasonable for you to seek couple therapy with the express goal of deciding whether or not to wed. You might choose to contract with a therapist for a limited time, say six sessions, or you might feel comfortable with a more open-ended arrangement. But, either way, all of you (the therapist, you, and your partner) could have an explicit understanding that dealing with the question of your marriage should be front and center.

What you can't know, though, is what issues might come up after you start. Perhaps as you explore the reasons for your reluctance to marry, you'll discover fundamental doubts about your partner's character. Or maybe you'll uncover some lingering feelings about your own parents' divorce that need working through. Because the path of your therapy is not predetermined, neither is its course.

Quite often, people decide to change the goals or focus of their therapy as it unfolds and new ideas and feelings come to the surface. At other times, they choose to end treatment when they've completed a piece of work or come to a better understanding of the issues. It will be the job of your therapist to help you assess, in an ongoing way, the progress you've made with respect to your goals and to offer you possibilities for future work. But it's up to you whether to go on.

> **Quite often, people decide to change the goals or focus of their therapy as it unfolds and new ideas and feelings come to the surface. At other times, they choose to end treatment when they've completed a piece of work or come to a better understanding of the issues.**

9. Someone might hold therapy against me in the future.

Your therapy is nobody's business but your own. Also, your therapist is bound by rules of professional confidentiality (see Chapter Nine).

However, it's true that health insurance companies can request reports from your therapist when considering payment, and health and life insurance companies can request reports when considering whether to underwrite new policies. Those records will then be stored in a database somewhere outside of your control. For some people, that breach of confidentiality is a reason to consider bypassing insurance and paying for therapy themselves, entirely out of their own pockets.

You can and should discuss with your therapist the proposed content of any communication she has with insurance companies or any other third party. Therapists have some leeway in what they write, and most can word their reports in a way that will be honest, ethical, and to the point, but not damaging to you. You should ask to see a copy of any letter or report written about you before it's sent.

10. Therapy doesn't work anyway.

Because the practice of psychotherapy is a "soft" rather than a "hard" science, it has sometimes come under attack as quackery. Some critics have argued that the success rate of therapy is no greater than that of spontaneous remission—in other words, patients would have gotten better on their own anyway. Others have argued that the benefits of therapy are due to the placebo effect. They claim it's the client's expectations that produce change, not the therapeutic process itself.

In recent years, especially as insurance companies have cracked down on longer-term therapy in favor of short-term treatment and medication, the mental health field has had to substantiate the efficacy of therapy. Research shows in fact that most people who work with a well-trained and skilled therapist experience significant benefits, regardless of the nature of their problems. In fact, therapy has been shown in many cases to reduce other health costs.

The data further suggests that the benefits of therapy will last longer if the goal is long-term change rather than short-term symptom relief. In other words, you're more likely to keep the gains you make if you've developed strategies for dealing with crises and stresses in the future.

Still have disturbing or puzzling questions about psychotherapy? Quite likely, you do. Making the decision to try therapy with a stranger, whether you've done it before or not, is a leap of faith that takes courage. If you're skeptical, discuss your doubts with the prospective therapist from the beginning. Remember: you're in the driver's seat, and you can always decide to drive away.

> **Making the decision to try therapy with a stranger, whether you've done it before or not, is a leap of faith that takes courage. If you're skeptical, discuss your doubts with the prospective therapist from the beginning. Remember: you're in the driver's seat, and you can always decide to drive away.**

PART TWO

The Lay of the Land

THREE

Important Theories

I KNOW THE mental health field can seem over-whelming to the outsider—so many different degrees, so many schools of thought, so many specialties. Plus, every day there seems to be a self-help guru touting the new "it" philosophy. How are you supposed to know where to begin? It's not important for you to be up on all the psychological literature or the new, hip treatments. By the time you finish this chapter, you'll have all the information you need to make a well-informed choice.

One of the reasons the mental health field can be confusing is that, since it encompasses so many different disciplines, there isn't a uniform set of terminology to describe its many categories and subcategories. Also, many terms have two meanings, one technical and one collo-quial, and we tend to apply them inconsistently. For example, a med-ical doctor could be correctly said to "specialize" in psychiatry and "subspecialize" in child psychiatry. But if she also does, say, couple ther-apy, we might describe her as "specializing" in that. And if she has a particular interest or expertise in eating disorders, we might even casually refer to those issues as her "specializations."

In order to understand how a therapist works and whether he is right for you, *you need to understand where he falls in each of five categories*. These categories are descriptive, not technical. If some of the terms sound daunting, don't be put off. They're actually commonsensical, and will be easy to understand once we define them. I'll do that briefly now, to orient you before we look at them in depth. Later, you'll be able to refer back to this list when you need to refresh your memory.

The Five Categories That Describe a Therapist

Theoretical Orientation

A practitioner's *theoretical orientation* is the school of thought in which she was trained (for example, psychodynamic or cognitive-behavioral), and it provides the guiding principles for her way of doing therapy. Of the five categories, this one will give you the most information about what it will be like to work with a particular mental health professional.

Professional Degree

Professional degree refers to the discipline in which a therapist originally qualified, such as psychiatry, social work, or psychology.

Modality/ies

The term *modality* simply refers to the type(s) of therapy that a professional provides, such as individual, couple, or family.

Specialized Technique/s

These are specific therapeutic methods that complement a clinician's basic general practice. *Specialized techniques*, such as EMDR (Eye Movement Desensitization and Reprocessing) and sex therapy, require additional training, and are extra tools in a therapist's toolbox.

Specialized Interest/s

Specialized interests are the topics in which a therapist has particular expertise, such as eating disorders, mood disorders, or addictions.

Because "theoretical orientation" is so important, we'll look at it separately here. We'll explore the other four categories in the next chapter.

Theoretical Orientation

Even the best mental health graduate programs can only offer an introduction to the art and science of therapy. Ethical clinicians know enough to supplement their original degrees with more training. They do this at therapist training schools, often called institutes. Institutes usually teach from a particular theoretical orientation. This theoretical orientation provides the framework for a clinician's practice—a way of thinking about patients, understanding their problems, and offering help.

If you've done any research into the different schools of therapeutic thought, you've probably felt overwhelmed by the dizzying array. Ego psychology, gestalt therapy, object relations therapy, existential therapy, rational-emotive therapy—the list goes on and on. What are the differences, and do you have to know? I don't think so. If you happen to have an interest in a particular theory, by all means read up on it (see "Suggestions for Further Reading," on pages 37–39). But while theoretical distinctions are important to us clinicians, you don't need a comprehensive knowledge of them. There are really only two basic ways of doing therapy: psychodynamic and cognitive/behavioral. Let's look at those two approaches in more detail.

The Psychodynamic Approach

Psychodynamic therapy has a number of different names, including "insight-oriented," "psychoanalytic," "exploratory," and the shortened term "dynamic" therapy. But they're all really focusing on an approach which focuses on understanding connections between past and present experience. Patients in this kind of treatment get relief by learning how their problems reflect patterns that were laid down earlier in their lives.

WHEN IS PSYCHODYNAMIC THERAPY A GOOD CHOICE?

Feeling better *now* is important in any therapy. But psychodynamic treatment also aims for substantial long-term growth. If you're interested in examining your inner life, this approach is for you.

ARE PSYCHODYNAMIC THERAPISTS AGAINST MEDICATION FOR EMOTIONAL PROBLEMS?

Most psychodynamic therapists believe talk therapy should be the first line of defense against most emotional problems, because medication alone doesn't usually produce profound or lasting results. However, all therapists agree medication is crucial in the treatment of certain disorders, such as suicidal depressions, bipolar illness, some severe anxieties, and schizophrenia. Also, most psychodynamic therapists will suggest medication to their patients who experience less severe but significant symptoms of depression and anxiety. Medication can actually be a good adjunct to talk therapy. Patients who are too depressed or anxious to explore their feelings can sometimes be enabled to do so with the support of medication.

WILL PSYCHODYNAMIC THERAPY WORK FOR PEOPLE IN CRISIS?

Many people have the misguided notion that psychodynamic therapy is not supportive. All good therapists know that to be helpful they must meet you where you *are*. If you come to therapy reeling from a recent loss, newly diagnosed with a serious illness, or having been physically assaulted, then you're in crisis. This isn't the time for you to be uncovering hidden conflicts. You need someone to help you focus on your strengths and mobilize whatever supports might be available to you. On the other hand, if your current trauma is reawakening feelings from earlier traumas in your life, you'll need a therapist who can help you make sense of that connection. Psychodynamic therapists can do both; they can attend to your need for support in the present while remaining sensitive to ways the past is being stirred up.

IS PSYCHODYNAMIC THERAPY ALWAYS LONG-TERM THERAPY?
No. The term *psychodynamic* refers to an approach, but not to a specific format. Many psychodynamic therapists will be happy to work with you on a short-term basis (perhaps six to twelve sessions) to resolve a specific problem. Some actually prefer short-term work, believing it motivates the patient and speeds up progress. A good therapist will let you know if your problem warrants longer-term attention.

The Cognitive/Behavioral Approach

Although cognitive and behavioral techniques aren't the same, we link them because they're usually practiced together. In contrast to psychodynamic therapists, cognitive/behavioralists aren't concerned with the unconscious or developing awareness and understanding. Rather than exploring transference, offering interpretations, and developing insight (for an explanation of these concepts see Chapter Five), cognitive/behavioral therapists focus on changing maladaptive patterns of thinking and behaving, and are actively directive in offering strategies for change.

Behavior therapy is closely linked to the concept of conditioning. We've all heard of Pavlov's dogs, which were trained to associate the sound of a bell with the presentation of food. Over time, the dogs salivated to the sound even when the food itself wasn't presented. For behaviorists, all human behavior (both emotional and physical) can be viewed as learned responses to environment. Behavioral therapy works by modifying responses that are maladaptive—in other words, these responses don't help the patient anymore. Its technique is based on the idea that when behaviors are rewarded they'll be repeated and when they're punished they won't. The behavior therapist makes a study of his patients' learned responses, and strives to extinguish negative ones and reinforce or elicit positive ones.

One of the better-known and most effective behavioral techniques is systematic desensitization, which is used to reduce the anxiety associated with certain situations. Patients with phobias can be helped by being exposed to their fears in progressive steps. Fear of riding in elevators, for example, might be approached by having the patient first imagine being in an elevator, then talk about riding in an elevator, then draw a picture of herself in an elevator, and finally trying the real thing.

Where behavior therapy focuses on learned behaviors, cognitive therapy focuses on learned thoughts, or cognitions. Proponents hold that emotional problems stem from irrational and self-defeating patterns of thinking, and they work actively to challenge patients' old belief systems and replace them with new ones. For example, if you told your cognitive therapist you felt rejected and inadequate because you'd been turned down for a job, your therapist might challenge your thinking by asking you to list all of the ways you behave competently, or all the people in your life who respect and look up to you.

WHEN IS COGNITIVE/BEHAVIORAL THERAPY A GOOD CHOICE?
Cognitive/behavioral therapies work well for the treatment of specific feelings and behaviors that have a fixed and irrational quality. Examples of these are:

- Phobias
- Obsessional thoughts
- Compulsive ritual behaviors (such as hand washing)
- Addictions
- Eating disorders
- Panic attacks
- Sexual dysfunctions

Cognitive/behavioral treatments alone, though, rarely produce lasting change. What usually works best for the symptoms listed above is a combination of psychodynamic and cognitive/behavioral techniques, and many well-trained therapists are good at using both.

There are a number of specific cognitive/behavioral treatments that are specializations in themselves and are often good adjuncts to psychodynamic therapy (see Chapter Four).

A HYPOTHETICAL INTERVIEW OF A PSYCHODYNAMIC THERAPIST AND A COGNITIVE/BEHAVIORAL THERAPIST

Question: What causes emotional problems?

The psychodynamic therapist responds: Painful experiences in the past shape the ways we continue to feel and behave in the present, even though we're often not aware of it. Our unconscious minds work to keep these painful memories, or at least the intense feelings that go along with them, out of our everyday thoughts. Symptoms such as anxiety, depression, phobias, or problems in relationships, are expressions of old conflicts we haven't fully faced and worked through. If we want to change, we have to deal with both the past and present.

The cognitive/behavioral therapist responds: It's our *thoughts and behaviors* that cause our emotional problems, not external factors like events, situations, or other people. If we're experiencing unwanted feelings or symptoms, it's because we've learned maladaptive or dysfunctional patterns of thinking and behaving in reaction to these external factors.

Question: How do patients get better?

The psychodynamic therapist responds: In the safe setting of therapy (which allows for taking risks) and the exploration of the relationship between the therapist and patient, we can make connections between what's happening now and what happened in the past. Change comes from dealing directly with our old painful feelings, and pairing them with new insights to develop better ways of coping.

The cognitive/behavioral therapist responds: Since most emotional and behavioral responses are learned, they can be unlearned. It's not necessary to examine the patient's past, or to understand his personality structure. Patients get better when they're helped to identify the thought and behavior patterns that cause their unwanted feelings, and then taught to replace them with thoughts and behaviors that lead to better reactions.

Question: How is therapy conducted?

The psychodynamic therapist responds: Therapy is a collaborative partnership. The therapist facilitates, guides, illuminates, and even explains—but mostly he follows the flow of his patient's thoughts and feelings without trying to direct them. Inevitably, this process leads the pair to the important issues that need attention. The therapeutic relationship is front and center. Its very existence makes the hard work possible, and it offers a laboratory for examining the patient's typical ways of relating. The therapy has some minimal structure (a fixed meeting time and place, and the like), but the therapist doesn't have an agenda or assign homework assignments. Therapy can be brief or long-term, depending on the patient's level of distress and the scope of his goals.

The cognitive/behavioral therapist responds: The therapist asks questions designed to help the patient identify specific goals, then implements a highly structured treatment plan. She doesn't tell her patient *what* these goals should be, but is directive in instructing him *how* to achieve them. She has an agenda for each session, which might involve a variety of techniques such as relaxation, EMDR, hypnosis, or systematic desensitization (see Chapter Four). She might supplement the sessions with homework or reading assignments. The therapeutic relationship is important, since therapy requires trust and collaboration, but it's not the focus of the work. The number of therapy sessions is limited, and the course is usually brief.

Okay, so which is better, psychodynamic therapy or cognitive/behavioral therapy? As I've said, the two are not mutually exclusive, and many clinicians use a combination of approaches. Still, there *is* a division in the mental health field over which is more legitimate. Practitioners on both sides can cite research supporting their point of view, although there's also research suggesting that, assuming the therapist is well trained, the approaches are equally effective.

The truth is that in debating psychodynamic versus cognitive/behavioral therapy we are really debating core beliefs and values—and these are the ones we hold onto no matter what a given study seems to show. Psychodynamic therapists believe that you can't treat a symptom as separate from the person as a whole. They value using the therapeutic relationship as a way of working through feelings and gaining understanding. Cognitive/behavioral therapists believe that you can treat a symptom without understanding its roots or working through the feelings associated with it. They favor active strategies for replacing maladaptive learned responses with better ones.

I've been doing this work long enough to have a healthy respect for many methods, and I present them here so you'll have a full range of options. But my bias is firmly in the psychodynamic camp. I do think cognitive/behavioral therapy works to relieve a number of specific problems, such as phobias and eating disorders. But in my experience, cognitive/behavioral treatments don't produce lasting, substantial change unless they're used along with psychodynamic talk therapy. And there's research to support this, too!

What's it like to be in psychodynamic therapy? How does it really help? In Chapter Five, "How Psychodynamic (or Insight-Oriented) Therapy Works," we'll take a look at those questions.

SUGGESTIONS FOR FURTHER READING

IF YOU'D like to know more about cognitive/behavioral or psychodynamic therapy, or about one of the other major schools of thought that are subsumed under those two categories, you might take a look at one of these books. Most of them were not intended for laypeople, but they're easily understood. Just read the parts that interest you.

Cognitive/Behavioral Therapy

- *Cognitive Therapy,* by Judith Beck (Guilford, 1995)
- *Handbook of Brief Cognitive Behavioral Therapies,* by Frank W. Bond and Windy Dryden, editors, (John Wiley and Sons, 2002)

- *Handbook of Cognitive-Behavioral Therapies, Second Edition,* by Keith Dobson, editor, (Guilford, 2002)

Ego Psychology

- *Ego Psychology,* by Gertrude and Rubin Blanck (Columbia University Press, 1992)

Existential Therapy

- *Existential Psychotherapy,* by Irvin Yalom (Basic Books, 1980)

Gestalt Therapy

- *The Gestalt Approach and Eye Witness to Therapy,* by Fritz Perls (Science and Behavior Books, 1980)

Object Relations Therapy

- *The Primer of Object Relations Therapy,* by Jill S. Scharff, M.D. and David E. Scharff, M.D. (Jason Aronson, 1995)

Psychodynamic Therapy

- *Inside Out and Outside In: Psychodynamic Clinical Theory and Practice in Contemporary Multicultural Contexts,* by Joan Berzoff, Laura Melano Flanagan, and Patrizia Hertz (Rowan and Littlefield, 2002)
- *Psychoanalytic Psychotherapy: A Practitioner's Guide,* by Nancy McWilliams (Guilford, 2004)
- *Freud and Beyond: A History of Modern Psychoanalytic Thought,* by Stephen A. Mitchell and Margaret J. Black (Basic Books, 1995)
- *The Gift of Therapy: An Open Letter to a New Generation of Therapists and Their Patients,* Irvin D. Yalom, M.D. (HarperCollins, 2002)

Rational/Emotive Therapy

- *A Practitioner's Guide to Rational-Emotive Therapy, Second Edition,* by Susan Walen, Raymond DiGiuseppe, and Windy Dryden (Oxford University Press, 1992)

Self Psychology

- *The Theory and Practice of Self Psychology,* by Marjorie Taggart White and Marcella Bakur Weiner (Brunner/Mazel, 1986)

Transpersonal Therapy

- *Going on Being: Buddhism and the Way of Change,* by Mark Epstein, M.D. (Broadway Books, 2001)
- *Integral Psychology: Consciousness, Spirit, Psychology, Therapy,* by Ken Wilbur (Shambhala, 2000)

Transactional Analysis

- *Games People Play: The Basic Handbook of Transactional Analysis,* by Eric Berne (Ballantine, 1996)

FOUR

Types of Therapists

NOW THAT WE'VE explored "theoretical orientation," we'll look more deeply into the other four categories that distinguish therapists from each other: professional degree, modality, special techniques, and special interests.

Professional Degree

A professional degree indicates that a therapist has qualified in one of the mental health disciplines (for example, social work or psychology), but it tells you very little about how he actually works. As I've already explained, most degree-granting programs don't adequately train their students to do therapy. Therefore a qualifying degree is really just a ticket into the mental health field. Once she's in, a conscientious therapist goes on to train further (see discussions of "institutes" in Chapter Seven). Unless you're looking for a service that can only be provided within a specific discipline (for example, only psychiatrists are qualified to prescribe psychotropic medications, and only psychologists can provide diagnostic testing), there's no need to seek out a therapist with a particular professional degree.

Since the field of psychotherapy isn't regulated by any umbrella agency, not all therapists are licensed. An unlicensed therapist isn't necessarily a quack. There are many well-qualified therapists in unlicensed fields, such as pastoral counseling. But there are benefits to choosing a licensed therapist. First, graduating in a licensed field means completing a rigorous course of study. This may or may not include some training in therapy, but it does indicate academic seriousness—a good thing in a helping professional. Second, licensed therapists must adhere to the standards of professional practice and ethics set by their state licensing board, and must submit to periodic review and relicensing. Third, insurance companies will only reimburse for therapy provided by licensed professionals. Fourth, only licensed professionals are eligible to purchase malpractice insurance, which is only relevant to you in the unlikely and unfortunate event that you have to sue them.

Licensed Professional Degrees

PSYCHIATRISTS (M.D.)
Psychiatrists are physicians. This means they've completed four years of medical school, one year of internship, and three years of residency training in psychiatry. Child psychiatrists have a minimum of four years of residency training, two in adult psychiatry and two in child psychiatry. Psychiatric training usually focuses primarily on the medical treatment of severe mental illness. In recent years, though, there has been greater focus on training in therapy, and some psychiatric residents complete their training with basic therapeutic competence.

About one-third of psychiatrists are board certified, which means they've passed an examination given by the American Board of Psychiatry and Neurology after three years of post-residency practice. However, since these exams focus primarily on issues around diagnosis and medical treatment of mental illness, board certification doesn't necessarily indicate an ability to do therapy. Membership in the American Psychiatric Association is a good sign but, like board certification, doesn't guarantee good therapy training.

As medical doctors, psychiatrists are the only mental health practitioners who can prescribe medication. Since an increasing number of psychiatrists are becoming psychopharmacologists (that is, working solely with the medical treatment of emotional disorders), be sure to ask if yours also does therapy and if she is appropriately trained to do so. We'll discuss medication issues further, later in this chapter.

PSYCHOLOGISTS (PH.D., PSY.D., ED.D)

Doctoral-level clinical psychologists usually have completed four years of graduate school plus a one-year internship. Besides clinical psychology, there are many other branches, including developmental, organizational, teaching, and social. Even within the clinical psychology training programs, many don't teach therapy but focus more on teaching their students to do diagnostic testing and research. A few, particularly those granting Psy.D.'s are more therapy-based.

Psychologists must complete a specified number of postdoctoral hours of supervised practice and pass a licensing examination before they can practice. Even though someone with any type of psychology degree can legally practice therapy, the American Psychological Association's code of ethics specifically requires its members to practice only in their area of expertise. The fact that a psychologist is a member of the American Psychological Association is a good sign that she adheres to a strict code of professional ethics, but it doesn't guarantee therapeutic skill.

Many psychologists do diagnostic testing in their practice. That is, they are qualified to administer specialized tests in such areas as personality, intelligence, and learning disabilities. Some of these testers will also be qualified therapists, but be sure to ask.

The fact that a practitioner has a Ph.D. doesn't necessarily mean he's a psychologist. Unless you ask, you'll have no way of knowing if your therapist's degree is in psychology or musicology!

Clinical social workers (M.S.W., C.S.W., L.C.S.W., L.I.C.S.W., A.C.S.W., D.S.W.)

Clinical social workers have completed either a master's or doctoral program in clinical social work. Like psychology, social work is a broad-ranging field, with its members working in the areas of social policy and research, social welfare and casework, and mental health. Depending on the academic focus of the school in which they were trained and the nature of their field placements (the "internship" part of their training) and supervision, new social workers will have more or less mental health experience. In order to be licensed, social workers must pass a state licensing exam in their area of professional concentration. Membership in The National Association of Social Workers indicates professional responsibility, but not therapeutic proficiency.

Psychiatric nurses (R.N.)

All states license nurses to practice, but there's no specialty or certification training in psychiatric nursing. In the past, psychiatric nurses worked only in mental hospitals. These days, some who have had specialized training also perform therapy in outpatient clinics. A few can prescribe medication under a doctor's supervision.

Licensed marriage and family therapists (L.M.F.T.)

Many states recognize and license this degree. Marriage and family therapists have typically completed a two-year master's program plus a minimum of two years of supervised practice in marriage and family therapy. Don't assume that a marriage and family therapist can't also do individual therapy; many have been trained in that, too—but you should check.

Licensed professional counselors (L.P.C.)

L.P.C.'s have a master's or doctoral degree in professional counseling or a related field and are certified and licensed by the American Counseling Association. Currently the license is recognized in forty-seven states. Some, but not all, insurance companies reimburse for therapy provided by L.P.C.'s, so you'll need to check with yours (see Chapter Six for a full discussion of insurance issues).

Unlicensed Professionals

PASTORAL COUNSELORS

Pastoral counselors are current or former members of the clergy who offer counseling or therapy services. Their preparation may be limited to that which they received in divinity school (some of which is very good), but many go on to do further therapy training. Before assuming a pastor has or hasn't been trained to provide the type of therapy you want, you should ask him about his background. And if religious or spiritual issues are important to you, a pastoral counselor with solid therapy training might be a good choice.

MASTERS-LEVEL PSYCHOLOGISTS

Even though most states don't license masters-level psychologists, there's nothing preventing them from getting training in or practicing therapy.

CAREER COUNSELORS AND LIFE COACHES

The International Coach Federation clearly states that coaching is *not* therapy. Coaches are more like consultants and cheerleaders; they help their clients define and achieve concrete goals. They're not concerned with the past or with developing new understanding. The field of coaching can be confusing, because some therapists are now also offering coaching services. If you see a coach for a consultation, be sure to ask exactly what his qualifications are and what services he's offering.

SUBSTANCE ABUSE COUNSELORS

There are many training programs in substance abuse counseling. If you're suffering with or in recovery from an addiction, seeing a substance abuse counselor could be important, either alone or as an adjunct to therapy. By and large, this group of counselors isn't well trained in therapy beyond the treatment of addictions.

Psychoanalysts (a special case)

Anyone who comes from one of the therapy disciplines and has been practicing high-level therapy can do psychoanalytic training to become an analyst. Although I'm not a psychoanalyst, psychoanalysis is near to my heart because it's the treatment I've found most effective in my own life. Unfortunately, most people are turned off by it because they think it's for the rich or crazy, or because they have outdated ideas about how psychoanalysts act. Yes, psychoanalysis was the invention of Freud, and not all his ideas have held up over time. But many of them, such as the importance of the unconscious and of early experience in shaping our mental lives, remain critically important today. Psychoanalysis has come a long way, and good practitioners these days are a far cry from the frightening caricature of the frigid "blank screen" analyst, whose stony silence in the face of the patient's outpourings of emotion is broken only by the scratching of his pen and an occasional "Mmmhmmm. . . ."

Psychoanalysis is an intensive form of therapy designed to produce profound and lasting change, and those who practice it have highly specialized and rigorous training. Patients in this form of treatment typically attend three to five sessions per week, usually for a minimum of two years, and most often lie on a couch. The analyst is highly attuned to the patient, but nondirective. The fact that analysts encourage the free flow of ideas in the patient (free association) has earned them the undeserved reputation of being cold and unresponsive. It's a shame that more people don't consider analysis as a viable therapeutic option. Despite the commitments of time and energy that psychoanalysis requires, it often brings the quickest relief and the deepest and most enduring changes. These days, it's often possible to obtain psychoanalysis at a low enough fee to make it affordable, sometimes from someone who is already an experienced therapist and is adding psychoanalysis to her set of therapy skills (see Chapter Seven).

Jungian analysts are a subset of analysts whose training and way of working are quite different from the others. Whereas classical analysts emphasize (though not exclusively) the influence of early experience on the development of later symptoms, Jungians are more interested in later life issues. Jungians focus on the psychological meaning of cross-cultural mythical ideas and images (called *archetypes*), which are carried in the patient's unconscious (particularly in dreams). Patients in Jungian analysis sit up in a chair (rather than lying on a couch) and typically attend one or two sessions per week.

Modality

Modality simply refers to the type of therapy that's being conducted, such as:

> Individual therapy
> Couple/Marital therapy
> Family therapy
> Child/Adolescent therapy
> Group therapy
> Psychoanalysis
> Medication therapy

Let's take a look at each at each of these.

Individual Therapy

WHEN TO CONSIDER INDIVIDUAL THERAPY:
- You suffer with a specific symptom (anxiety, depression, phobia) from which you want relief.
- You're troubled by ineffective or self-defeating patterns of behavior in a number of areas of your life.
- You feel your problems require one-on-one support from a therapist.
- You feel your problems originate within you.
- You feel you need couple or family therapy, but your partner or family refuses to go.

Limitations to individual therapy

When there are difficulties in relationships, it's common for those problems to be mistakenly viewed as existing only in one person. For example, a family that's having a lot of trouble with intimacy among and between its members may experience itself as having one very difficult child, say an acting-out adolescent. When this happens we say that one person, the "identified patient," is "containing" the problems of the whole family, because it's more difficult for the family to face the complexities of its problems than to think of itself as having one troubled member. If you or another person in your family is "containing" problems that are really shared by everyone, then individual therapy will only reinforce the problem. A good therapist will know when couple or family therapy is indicated in order to help others take ownership of a shared problem.

Couple/Marital Therapy

When to consider couple/marital therapy:

- You and your partner agree that your relationship needs work.
- You or your partner haven't benefited from individual therapy.
- Your therapist or your partner's therapist feels your problem is a couple problem.
- One of you has been in individual therapy and the other is having trouble adjusting to resulting changes in the relationship.
- Couple therapy is the only way to get your partner to see a therapist.
- You both need therapy but you can't afford two individual therapists.
- You have sexual difficulty that may be related to a difficulty in the relationship.

Note: Even though we often colloquially refer to a therapist who works with couples as a "couples therapist," that's like calling someone a "families therapist." The correct term is "couple therapist."

Family Therapy

WHEN TO CONSIDER FAMILY THERAPY:

- As a parent, you feel out of control of the family's functioning.
- There's a lot of fighting and unhappiness in the family.
- One or more of the children seem to be running things.
- Everyone agrees the family needs help.
- One or more members of the family are in individual therapy, and it isn't working.
- One or more members of the family need therapy, but you have limited financial resources.
- One member of the family is in individual therapy, and other members of the family are having difficulty adjusting to changes.
- The family is having trouble facilitating the separation of an older child who is ready to leave home.
- One or more of your children feel they're being unfairly treated.

Child/Adolescent Therapy

We'll discuss child and adolescent therapy in some length in Chapter Eleven. The important thing to remember is that while many therapists do this type of therapy, not all are trained in it. Make sure to ask about the training of any therapist whom you hire to work with your child.

Group Therapy

Theoretical approaches to group therapy vary. Sometimes they're problem-focused; members share a common difficulty, such as eating disorders or phobias. At other times they're more general; members bring the normal range of issues that all patients bring to therapy. Group therapy can be extremely effective in helping you understand the ways your relationships are stuck or frozen, and helping you gain a broader range of relating styles. In a group, your typical modes of behavior come powerfully to life, and you have a rich, here-and-now opportunity to explore them. Members learn from each other as well as the therapist, as they experiment with new ways of being together in the safe therapeutic environment. Group therapy can be an effective stand-alone treatment, or an excellent adjunct to individual work.

WHEN TO CONSIDER GROUP THERAPY:
- You have trouble making or keeping friends.
- You have trouble with authority.
- You're shy or inhibited.
- People say you're difficult to get along with.
- You're lonely.
- You're afraid of intimacy.
- You have trouble asserting yourself.
- Individual therapy hasn't been effective.

Psychoanalysis

WHEN TO CONSIDER PSYCHOANALYSIS:
- Your problems are longstanding and/or far-reaching.
- You're highly motivated.
- You want to make substantive and long-lasting changes in your life.
- Less intensive therapy hasn't helped.
- Less intensive therapy has helped, but you want to take your treatment to a new level.
- Your therapist suggests you could benefit from psychoanalysis.

Medication

The question of when to consider psychotropic (psychiatric) medications is one of the most controversial topics in the mental health field. There's always been some disagreement between talk therapists and those who adhere to a medical model of mental illness, but it's been exacerbated in recent years by insurance companies' promoting of medication as a quicker and cheaper cure. Medication is crucial in the treatment of serious mental illnesses, such as schizophrenia, bipolar disorder, and severe forms of anxiety and depression.

It can also be helpful in the treatment of more common problems such as mild or moderate anxiety and depression, or obsessive-compulsive symptoms. But no pill alone can solve the complexities of emotional distress. Studies clearly show that medication is most effective when it's used in combination with talk therapy.

The decision to try medication for emotional distress is a personal one, so don't feel you have to do it just because your therapist says so. If you have doubts, consider getting a second opinion or waiting to see if symptoms resolve in therapy. Though some patients report miraculous results from medication, some experience a diminishing benefit over time. And others report no benefit at all. Also, most medications have side effects, which can range from moderate to severe. Still, if you have persistent symptoms that cause you significant distress, medication could help. It might even facilitate your work in therapy by taking the distracting edge off your discomfort.

IF YOU WANT TO CONSIDER MEDICATION:

- Take the time to find an experienced psychiatrist who is up on current medications (new and better drugs come on the market all the time).
- Don't hire someone who's willing to prescribe drugs without first getting to know you and your specific problems. A good psychiatrist will take a comprehensive history in your first one or two meetings.
- Don't hire a psychiatrist unless she insists on seeing you, in person, to check on your progress. Meetings should be more frequent in the beginning (say, once or twice a month), and less frequent (but still regular) as you stabilize on medication.
- Be sure to ask about the potential side effects of any drugs that your psychiatrist prescribes.
- Ask if and how you will be able to contact your psychiatrist in case of emergency, or if you feel any ill effects from your medication.
- Be sure to ask how long your psychiatrist thinks you will need to take the medication. Will there be a plan for

stopping if symptoms abate, or will you be taking medication indefinitely?

- Be sure to ask if the drug tends to lose its efficacy over time. If so, what will be the plan?
- Some medications are addictive. Be sure to ask about the potentially addictive qualities of any medications that you're prescribed.
- If you have any ill effects from the medication or feel it's not helping, don't stop taking it without first speaking with your psychiatrist. Many side effects resolve after a few days or weeks, and many medications must be taken for several weeks before they become effective. Also, stopping a medication suddenly can cause its own problems.
- Use the same criteria for choosing a medicating psychiatrist that you would for choosing any other therapist (see Chapter Six). Find someone who's willing to spend the time it takes to get to know you and respond to any questions or concerns you have. Don't settle for someone with an overly busy practice who sees patients for a cursory five or ten minutes. If you feel you're being treated "like a number," go elsewhere.

SUGGESTIONS FOR FURTHER READING

IF YOU'D like to learn more about psychiatric medications, take a look at one or more of these books:

- "If You Need Medication," in *The Consumer's Guide to Psychotherapy,* by Jack Engler and Daniel Goleman (Simon and Schuster, 1992)
- *The Essential Guide to Psychiatric Drugs,* by Jack M. Gorman (St. Martin's Press, 1995)
- *Listening to Prozac,* by Peter D. Kramer (Penguin Books, 1997)
- Chapters 5–11 in *Straight Talk About Your Mental Health,* by James Morrison (Guilford, 2002)
- *Straight Talk About Psychiatric Medications for Kids,* by Timothy E. Wilen (Guilford, 2002)

Specialized Techniques

These days there are more ways than ever for therapists to expand their repertoires. While there will always be new flash-in-the-pan gimmicks, there are many specialized techniques that are firmly rooted in solid clinical and theoretical thinking. As I've said, though, even the best of these is most helpful when used is conjunction with more general talk therapy. Outside of a therapeutic relationship, they're not as effective.

Some Important Specialized Techniques

EMDR

Eye Movement Desensitization and Reprocessing (EMDR) is a treatment for those who suffer the lingering emotional effects of trauma. This treatment is relatively new and still quite controversial. But it's gaining popularity even among the mainstream of therapists, many of whom claim it produces dramatic results in a short time. EMDR is based on the idea that memories of overwhelmingly traumatic experiences have been forced out of consciousness, yet remain locked within a person's nervous system, and that people who suffer such symptoms as flashbacks, depression, and anxiety related to these experiences can be helped if these neural traces can be released and transformed into less problematic forms.

The technique of EMDR involves having the patient mentally visualize the traumatic experience or event while visually tracking a light that is moving side to side or following a rhythmic sound (such as tapping). Practitioners claim EMDR neurologically reactivates the original traumatic experience, and allows for the detoxification of this experience in the present.

Sex therapy

The best sex therapists approach sexual problems from both a psychodynamic and behavioral angle. They know that sex, like every other important area of human relating, is highly influenced by our unconscious thoughts and feelings and our past experiences, both good and bad. They also know that some sexual dysfunctions have medical, rather than psychological, roots. A well-trained sex therapist will first rule out a medical problem, and then help you design a treatment that addresses both the intrapsychic (within you) and interpersonal (between you and your partner) aspects of your problem. This treatment will involve both talk therapy and behavioral exercises to help you learn better patterns of sexual relating.

HYPNOTHERAPY

In the past, hypnosis was touted as a method of regaining access to repressed (pushed out of awareness) memories, but this use has been discarded. These days, hypnosis, or hypnotherapy, has gained respect as a way of helping people get in touch with and learn to tolerate *feelings* associated with past traumatic events. Hypnotherapists typically use a series of "guided imagery" exercises, in which the patient reexperiences the sensory memories associated with the trauma.

This work bears little resemblance to the theatrical form of the art practiced by stage hypnotists. In reality, you can't be hypnotized to perform acts against your will or to disclose information you'd prefer to keep to yourself.

BIOFEEDBACK

Biofeedback is a technical process that helps people learn to manage chronic pain, such as migraines. Patients are connected to a machine that monitors their physical responses (such as a rise or fall in blood pressure or heart rate, or a tensing of muscles). The machine signals any changes in these processes. Once patients have become attuned to these changes, they can learn techniques such as relaxation, breathing, and visualization techniques to help control them.

DIALECTICAL BEHAVIOR THERAPY (DBT)

DBT is a subset of cognitive/behavioral therapy that encompasses an array of techniques. It is used to treat people who have difficulties regulating their emotions. Patients of therapists who use this type of treatment are typically quite depressed or anxious (sometimes suicidal), angry, disorganized, and chaotic. DBT emphasizes "dialectics," that is, the reconciliation of opposites. The most central of these dialectics is that patients must be accepted as they are, but in a context of teaching them to change. The DBT practitioner validates the "grain of truth" even in the patient's most outrageous perceptions and responses, while actively teaching such skills as emotion regulation, interpersonal effectiveness, distress tolerance, and self-management. The therapy entails individual treatment, skills training (often in groups), and telephone consultation.

ART, MUSIC, AND DRAMA THERAPIES

These so-called "expressive therapies" use the creative arts as a medium for the expression and working through of emotional problems. Therapists in private practice rarely limit their work to the expressive therapies, although some use them as effective adjuncts to traditional talk therapy.

BODY THERAPY

Body therapy is an offshoot of the main group of therapies, and is based on the idea that we are *embedded* in our physical selves. That is, our minds and our bodies are inextricably linked. Body therapists believe that all experience, as well as our own ways of distorting and defending against it, is reflected not only in our minds but also in the ways that the structure of our bodies evolves. There are many different approaches to body therapy. Techniques might include: meditation to help the client get in touch with her bodily sensations, exercises to help the client become more expressive (such as kicking, making sounds, reaching, moving toward another person, eye movements), movements to help the client get more in touch with his body, ways to deepen breathing, and therapeutic touch where agreed upon and appropriate. Clients seek body therapy for the same reasons they seek any therapy, but also for physical problems such as headaches and lower-back pain. The United States Association for Body Psychotherapy stresses that the therapeutic relationship is as critical in body therapy as in any other type. In other words, body therapists must be fully qualified talk therapists *first*.

Special Interests

Some therapists focus on a narrow area of clinical work, either exclusively or as part of a general practice. If you have a specialized issue (such as an eating disorder, a phobia, or a sexual problem) and want a therapist who specializes in it, fine. But be careful: in today's market, where more therapists are vying for fewer patients, many have developed special interests principally as "hooks" for attracting business. There's nothing wrong with that, as long as the therapist is well qualified. But the fact that a therapist advertises herself as a specialist doesn't guarantee she's had special training in that area. Be sure to ask.

Some so-called specialties are really just gimmicks, or fancy repackaging of old ideas. If you're a woman you don't need a therapist specializing in women's issues, and if you're a business executive you don't need one specializing in "the treatment of today's busy professional." In general, steer clear of the glitz and go for the tried and true.

And the fact that therapists don't need to tout themselves as being specialists per se doesn't mean they're not equipped to help. Clinicians with many years of experience will have seen a broad range of patients with different types of problems—so you should ask if they're comfortable with your problem and feel they can work with you. Above all, you want someone who won't try to fit you into the neat package, but who'll take the time to get to know your unique qualities. A special area of interest shouldn't narrow a therapist's focus so much that she misses seeing you as a whole person, for whom, for example, an eating disorder is the sign of other things you could use help with.

Now we can review a list of special therapy interests. Obviously this list can't be exhaustive, but it'll give you a sense of the range of available options.

SOME IMPORTANT AREAS OF SPECIAL INTEREST:
- Geriatrics
- Eating disorders
- Mood disorders (including anxiety, depression, and manic-depression)

- Obsessive-compulsive disorder
- Developmental disorders (such as autism and Asperger's syndrome, which span many developmental problems in children)
- Addictions
- Phobias
- Psychotic disorders (such as schizophrenia)
- Trauma (both physical and emotional)
- Gender-identity disorders
- Dissociative disorders (such as multiple personality disorder)
- Learning problems
- Attention deficit hyperactive disorder (in children or adults)
- The psychological effects of medical illness and chronic pain
- Sexual problems
- Sports psychology
- Sexual abuse
- Domestic violence
- Gay/lesbian issues
- Divorce/child custody issues
- Forensics (mental health and the law)

FIVE QUESTIONS TO ASK ANY NEW THERAPIST

What's your theoretical orientation?

This will tell you what school of thought a therapist works from. If the therapist is too general ("Oh, I'm sort of eclectic") or too specific ("I'm an ego-psychologist with a smattering of gestalt and existential"), tell him you have no idea what he's talking about and want to know if he's basically psychodynamic or cognitive/behavioral. Many therapists use a combination of approaches, and that's fine, but the good ones can explain their work clearly anyway.

What's your professional degree?

This will tell you whether the therapist is, for example, a social worker, a psychologist, or a psychiatrist. A therapist's degree tells you less about her than do the types of training she's had *since* earning it.

What modalities do you work in?

This will tell you whether a clinician is an individual, couple, family, child, or group therapist, or only prescribes medication. Many therapists work in multiple modalities, but that doesn't guarantee they've had the requisite training. Be sure to ask.

Do you employ any special techniques in your practice?

This will tell you if the therapist only does talk therapy, or if he has had supplementary training in an alternate way of working, such as hypnotherapy. Remember: special techniques can complement your therapy, but they can't substitute for it.

Do you have any areas of special interest or expertise?

This will tell you if there are any areas of practice in which the therapist has special training or experience, such as domestic violence or eating disorders. The fact that a therapist doesn't advertise herself as specializing in the problem for which you're seeking help doesn't necessarily mean she couldn't work effectively with you.

FIVE

How Psychodynamic (or Insight-Oriented) Therapy Works

First, the Qualities Common to All Good Therapies

The word *therapy,* as used here, is actually a shortened form of the word psychotherapy, which means any treatment aimed at helping the patient or client resolve an emotional, behavioral, or interpersonal problem. The goal might be to eliminate or reduce a symptom (such as a phobia or feelings of sadness or anxiety), or to improve functioning in any number of areas (such as relationships or work). Sometimes people come to therapy simply to understand themselves better so they can make better choices. Most often, the goal is some combination of all of these.

Most therapists do "talk therapy." That is, the way we come to understand and help you is through a dialogue. Each of us has our own way of understanding your problem and of being helpful, which comes from our unique combination of background, training, and personal style. Not all therapists confine their work to "talk therapy." Some employ other techniques, such as those I described in Chapter Four.

All therapists worth their salt, no matter what "school" they were trained in, know that their most important tool is their relationship with you. At first, the therapeutic relationship may seem strange and artificial. After all, it's unlike any other you've known. You and your therapist won't be friends, although you'll have fond, even loving feelings for each other. You won't be lovers, although you may have sexual feelings for your therapist at one time or another. You won't be teacher and student; you'll learn from each other.

> **All therapists worth their salt, no matter what "school" they were trained in, know that their most important tool is their relationship with you.**

The therapeutic relationship is a collaborative partnership. Like any good partnership, it can't be established instantly. It forms as you both get to know each other, sometimes over just a few sessions, sometimes over years. But regardless of its life span, to be successful it must have certain components. They are:

- The frame
- The approach
- Nonjudgmental listening
- Trust
- Caring
- Empathy
- A good fit between therapist and client

Now let's look at each of these components individually.

The Elements of the Therapeutic Relationship

THE FRAME

Any good parent knows that children thrive on routine. When their lives follow certain organized principles, they feel safe and secure. This is true on both the concrete and the emotional levels. Kids do best when mealtimes and sleep cycles are fairly regular, and when the important people in their lives are consistently present and behave in emotionally predictable ways. When their lives are going well, when they can trust that the adults taking care of them will be available when they're needed, children can tolerate normal amounts of chaos and disappointment. But when their lives are unpredictable and the adults in their lives are unreliable, children become anxious and disorganized. Structure, when it's thoughtfully imposed, provides clear boundaries in which kids can do the playful work of childhood. In other words, it frees them up to be themselves.

Therapy works in very much the same way as good parenting; it must have a thoughtful and consistent (but not punitive or inflexible) structure to be effective. This structure is called the therapeutic frame. The therapeutic frame is both like the frame of a house (providing the walls and beams that support the structure) and like the frame of a painting (providing the outline for the creative work).

ASPECTS OF THE THERAPEUTIC FRAME

Setting
Your therapy should take place in an appropriately organized, professional office. This office could be in an office building, a hospital, a clinic, or a private home. It's not important that you love the décor, but the space should be inviting. There should be a comfortable chair for you and another for the therapist, a reasonable conversational distance away. And the space should be private; you shouldn't have to worry that your session will be interrupted by telephone calls or that other patients in the waiting room can overhear you.

Meeting Time
You're entitled to a scheduled time that's regular and predictable. Some rescheduling to suit you or your therapist is inevitable, but should be the exception rather than the rule. Even if, because of special life considerations, you and your therapist have decided not to have a fixed appointment time but to schedule sessions as you go, the therapist should keep to the agreed time.

Length of Session

In general, a standard therapy session is forty-five or fifty minutes. Some (especially in family and couple therapy) may last a full hour or longer. You should know, before a session starts, how long it will be, and every session should be the same length unless you prearrange otherwise.

Frequency

You and your therapist should determine how frequently you'll come, and strive to maintain that frequency whenever possible. Some people benefit from weekly sessions, but others may need more intensive work, either because their distress is intense, or because their goals for change are more ambitious. A few patients can manage with less than one session per week, but usually only if they have already been in therapy for some time or have very modest goals.

Fee

Your therapist should tell you before you start how much you will be charged for sessions, when you will receive your bill, and when and how you are to pay.

THE APPROACH

As I explained in Chapters Three and Four, there are many legitimate approaches to therapy. Your clinician should be well trained in an approach or combination of approaches that he can explain to you. His technique shouldn't be a mystery.

NONJUDGMENTAL LISTENING

Therapists are just people, and of course they have reactions and opinions. By and large, though, they should keep these to themselves. You're the one who has to make your own choices and decisions, and you should feel free to be honest about things without having your therapist second-guessing you or telling you what to do. The exception is if you're engaged in a self-destructive activity (such as drunk driving). In that case, it would be irresponsible of your therapist to stay neutral. But there's a big difference between calling your attention to a self-destructive behavior, in order to get you to think about it, and sitting in judgment on it. A good therapist is not a moral arbiter.

TRUST

You want someone you can trust. Even the best therapists are sometimes late for appointments, get distracted, or say something that indicates they don't understand you at that moment. The good ones are open to being corrected. They welcome confrontation and don't get angry or retaliate when you criticize them. For your treatment to succeed, you have to believe your therapist has your best interests in mind and is acting in good faith.

CARING

Even though therapy is a business relationship with a particular structure, it's still an important, real, and caring one. A good therapist is nonjudgmental, but not detached. Even though all clients get angry at or frustrated with their clinicians at times (what close relationship does not contain these elements?), they care about them. And they are cared for in return.

EMPATHY

No one but you can ever really know what it's like to be you. But a good therapist, in addition to being warm and caring, should make every effort to understand what it means to walk in your shoes. The capacity to enter into your experience, to understand you on a gut level, is critical. Therapists call this *empathy*, and they've had years of training enabling them to develop it. You want an empathic therapist who "gets" you.

A GOOD FIT

In therapy, as in life, one size doesn't fit all. Studies have shown that therapy is most successful when patients play an active role in selecting a therapist whose personality and way of working are a good match with their own. Find someone you feel comfortable with (see Chapter Seven).

Now, the Qualities of Psychodynamic Therapy

Psychodynamic therapy is based on the idea that at any one time we're only aware of a small part of what's going on in our minds. The part of us driving the way we think, feel, and behave, without our conscious awareness, we call the "unconscious." Our unconscious minds wield a lot of power over us. If you've ever had a disturbing dream that brought to the surface of your thoughts something you hadn't been thinking about before, if you've ever made a "Freudian slip," or "accidentally" forgotten a meeting that deep-down you wanted to avoid, then you've seen the evidence.

The unconscious is crucial in therapy because it holds the secret of our life difficulties. Bad things do happen, yes. People die, parents get divorced, husbands leave, friends treat us poorly, we lose our jobs. And life itself is demanding. Our careers require more and more of our time, parenting is a tricky business, care for elderly parents is exhausting and baffling, marriage is hard work. Usually, though, when we have trouble coping with life, what's getting in the way is mainly ourselves. Rather, it's that pesky part of ourselves that works against change to maintain our own emotional status quos. And if you think about it, this makes sense. Every way we feel, every way we behave, every fear we suffer made sense at one point in our lives.

> **When we have trouble coping with life, what's getting in the way is mainly ourselves. Rather, it's that pesky part of ourselves that works against change to maintain our own emotional status quos. And if you think about it, this makes sense. Every way we feel, every way we behave, every fear we suffer made sense at one point in our lives.**

Let's take the example of Sally.

Sally is an overspender; no matter how much money she earns, she spends twice as much. She doesn't really need the things she buys. But whenever there's money in her pocket she feels the overwhelming urge to drive to the mall to buy clothes, jewelry, or makeup. When she buys these things, she feels immediate relief. But soon after, she's filled with remorse. She hides her loot from her family. Her husband is angry with her for spending money that would be better spent on other things. He demands she stop, and threatens to leave when she can't. Sally feels awful—depressed, ashamed, and worried about her marriage and her financial future.

Sally grew up in a financially strapped family of eight children, with two working and overwhelmed parents. While Sally's grown-up self says she doesn't need to spend money in this irresponsible way, there's another part of her, a younger part, still feeling needy and deprived. That younger part of her lives in the past, in a time when she had to compete with her siblings for her parents' love and attention. In order to get her share of the family's emotional resources she had to fight for them. That is, she had to "steal" them from someone else. That left her feeling not only deprived, but guilty.

Sally's strategy of actively competing with her brothers and sisters made sense in the context of her childhood. As an adult, she no longer needs this coping strategy. In fact, it's destructive. But the young, deprived version of herself lives on in her unconscious mind, still acting in the same old ways. Now she hoards things not because she needs them, but in an effort to soothe old feelings of deprivation.

There are as many possible explanations for overspending as there are people who do it. But the point is that a cycle of feeling and behavior that made sense early in life can persist later in ways that hold us back from functioning as our best selves. In therapy, you can gain access to the unconscious parts of yourself that make you unhappy or cause you to shoot yourself in the foot.

Tapping Into the Unconscious: Free Association

So how can you get access to your unconscious? In psychodynamic therapy you'll be asked to say aloud whatever comes into your mind, with as little censorship as possible. This process is called "free association." What comes into your mind might be a disagreement that morning with a colleague at work, it might be the memory of your seventh birthday party, it might be a dream, or it might simply be a feeling. But as you follow the idea or feeling, and allow your mind to play with it to see what occurs to you, you'll learn a lot about yourself and the problem that brought you there.

The idea of simply saying whatever comes into your mind might seem pointless, or inefficient. After all, if you're coming to therapy because you're dissatisfied with your job but are having trouble deciding what job you would like to try, you'll naturally want to talk about new career ideas. But if you're unhappy at work, chances are you've already thought about lots of job options. And, after all, you may have friends or trusted family members who can give you advice and help you weigh the advantages and disadvantages of various possibilities. Even though it might seem irrelevant to talk about the movie you saw last night, if that's what's on your mind, talk about it. You never know, you may discover that the movie has lingered in your thoughts because one of the characters reminds you of a fearful aspect of yourself that you hadn't been consciously thinking about. And perhaps that aspect is related to your work problems. The point is, unless you explore you'll never know which path could lead to important discoveries.

Naturally, you can't talk about everything that pops into your mind. There's only so much time in a session, and no one can completely avoid self-censoring. Free association is really an ideal concept, something to aspire to. It's not something you can ever fully achieve. Also, the term *free association* comes from psychoanalysis, not therapy (for an explanation of the difference, see Chapter Four). It's easier to free-associate in psychoanalysis because the patient faces away from the analyst (so is less distracted), attends more frequent sessions (so has less news to report), and lies on a couch (so is more relaxed). But even in ordinary therapy there are some ways to help yourself come close to free association:

STICK WITH YOUR FIRST THOUGHT

Lots of patients start to talk about something , then stop themselves with a "never mind, that's not important." When they do, I usually encourage them to continue with their original train of thought. Consider this excerpt from a session with Laura, a woman I've been treating for some time:

LAURA: Sorry I'm late. What a day. Oh my god. Never mind. What were we talking about last time?

KATE: You seem flustered.

LAURA: Oh, it's been one thing after another. Anyway, weren't we talking about the kids? How I need to set stricter limits with them?

KATE: You want to pick up where we left off, but you're upset about something right now.

LAURA: Oh, it's not important. It's silly. It's just that when I was driving here, on the highway, this lady in a big SUV almost cut me off. She wasn't looking at all, she just veered right into my lane. But when I honked at her, she gave me the finger. I couldn't believe it. I was just letting her know I was there. But she acted like I was the one who had done something wrong!

KATE: You're pretty upset about it.

LAURA: Well, yeah. I mean, she had no right to flip me off like that.

KATE: It really got to you.

LAURA: It did. And you know, *that's* what really upsets me. She was just some bitch on the highway, maybe just having a bad day, or something. But I feel all riled up about it. Like my whole mood is ruined.

KATE: Your reaction feels out of proportion.

LAURA: Yeah. I don't get it.

(Several moments of silence)

KATE: You were trying to protect yourself, and she got angry at you for it.

LAURA: Yes. That's like my father, isn't it? It's like when he'd drink and yell at me. I was afraid, but if I yelled back at him he'd get so angry!

GO WHERE YOUR FEELINGS LEAD

My clue that something important had happened to Laura was that she was clearly carrying a lot of feelings. I followed them, and we got to the incident on the highway. On the surface, it was a mundane episode. What made it significant was *her* experience of it, its meaning *to her*. Even if a topic seems unremarkable at first, if you have powerful emotions related to it, it's bound to be important.

The therapy technique of paying close attention to and following a patient's feelings is called "following the affect."

> **Even if a topic seems unremarkable at first, if you have powerful emotions related to it, it's bound to be important.**

PUSH YOURSELF TO SHARE PAINFUL OR EMBARRASSING THOUGHTS

We all have skeletons in our closets—memories, feelings, and ideas that cause us shame. And we all have "hot topics" that cause us discomfort; for some of us it's sex, for others money or something else. Your therapy will go best if you push yourself to open up. If you don't, your emotional problems will likely "hide out" in the areas you don't discuss and compromise the rest of your therapy.

> **We all have "hot topics" that cause us discomfort; for some of us it's sex, for others money or something else. Your therapy will go best if you push yourself to open up. If you don't, your emotional problems will likely "hide out" in the areas you don't discuss and compromise the rest of your therapy.**

For example, say you're in treatment for depression, and also suffer from impotence. Your inability to perform sexually is so humiliating to you that you can't bring yourself to discuss it with your therapist. In sessions, you explore the reasons for your depression. You come to understand its roots, and you make progress in certain areas. For example, work is going well, and you feel less sad than you used to. But you've plateaued in therapy; you can't seem to really feel *good*. You're stuck.

Because you haven't talked about your impotence, it continues to be a problem. Your relationship with your partner is suffering. To make matters worse, the fact that you've kept the issue from your therapist has made you feel dishonest and guilty. The longer you keep it to yourself, the harder it feels to bring it up. Now you feel not only ashamed of the impotence, but also of your fear.

There's a lot of truth to the old adage that "we're only as sick as our secrets." Once you bring them into the light of day, those things about yourself that seem horrible and shameful will be much easier to tolerate. They'll also be available to be worked on and changed. If there's a topic that you really can't bring yourself to discuss—it's just too embarrassing or painful—start small. Tell your therapist that there's something on your mind, but you're not ready to talk about it. That way, the issue is on the table, and your therapist can support your efforts to open it up.

Transference

Many people think of psychodynamic therapists as cold and silent. Not true. Good therapists of any ilk are warm and empathic. But the psychodynamic ones do aim for a special kind of neutrality. They're not neutral about *you*: they care about you and want you to do well. This kind of neutrality means they don't impose an agenda. The key to successful psychodynamic treatment lies in understanding the painful thoughts and feelings that have been hidden away in your unconscious, and the only way to get to those is by following your own train of thought. It's the job of the therapist, then, to provide a safe emotional space, to offer guidance, and to help you develop your own insights.

You may wonder why therapists tend to be a bit close-mouthed about their own lives. Often, they won't offer information about their marital status, religion, whether they have children, and the like. They may not answer if you ask them a direct question such as, "What do you think I should do?" or "Don't you think that was a terrible thing my mother did to me?" Therapists are only human, and you'll glean many of their characteristics and personality traits over time, whether they like it or not. But too much information about your therapist and her opinions will get in the way. Why? Because of *transference,* a central concept in psychodynamic therapy.

When we meet someone new, we don't react neutrally. Even when we simply pass strangers on the street our minds register them in a thousand different ways. We might think, "Oh, she's so beautiful, she probably wouldn't look twice at me," or "He looks like he's having a bad day—better stay away." When we form relationships, we cope with our natural anxiety by gauging the ways the new person does or doesn't conform to the familiar. Thoughts like: "He's funny, like my brother" or "She isn't Catholic, so she probably won't like me" help us navigate new territory. When we attribute to one person or situation the qualities or characteristics of another person or situation, that's transference at work. Transference is by no means a bad thing. In fact, it often draws people together. Most people choose their spouses based on a familiar resonance.

On the other hand, through transference we can perpetuate old patterns of feeling and behavior that don't serve us well. For example, if you had an uncaring father, you may experience some of your male friends that way, when they're only guilty of being men you're close to. The problem will be complicated further if you angrily accuse them of not caring about you. They'll withdraw, thereby confirming your fears, and you'll be locked in an unconscious cycle that replicates your early unhappy experiences with your father.

A psychodynamic therapist's neutrality encourages your transference feelings—both positive and negative—to come out. It also allows you to explore these feelings more easily than if they were muddied up by your therapist's actual character and points of view. Your relationship with your therapist is like a controlled, concentrated version of all your other relationships (past and present), and you can learn a tremendous amount about yourself by studying it.

> **Your relationship with your therapist is like a controlled, concentrated version of all your other relationships (past and present), and you can learn a tremendous amount about yourself by studying it.**

Interpretations and Working Through

People usually think of an interpretation as something smart a therapist tells his patient. And that's not wrong. Part of an interpretation is an explanation, a connection between your past experience and your present life. In the example I gave about Sally the overspender, the interpretation is that overspending in the present alleviates the terrible feeling of deprivation Sally felt as an overlooked child in an overtaxed family. But if I had offered this interpretation to Sally at the very beginning of our work together, it wouldn't have been too helpful. She might have agreed with the interpretation, either because she had thought of it before on her own, or because it felt true. But the interpretation would only have been based on a superficial understanding of Sally, and it would have affected her only superficially. In other words, it might have made intellectual sense, but it wouldn't have gone in on a gut level.

What I did first was allow a relationship to develop. Then, in the context of our therapeutic connection, Sally was able repeatedly to get in touch with the strong feelings of sadness, anger, frustration, and guilt she had about her overspending. It was those feelings, which our relationship helped her to bear, that led Sally to make her own connections between her past and present experience.

You might know someone who's been thoroughly "therapized." He's seen lots of shrinks, and he's able to sum himself up in a neat nutshell. He knows himself inside out; by now he has a script. So what? He's still a pain in the neck. The reason he can't change is that his insights are all intellectual. As I explained in the Introduction, therapy isn't so much about ideas as it is about feelings. A new insight from your therapist might be interesting, but it won't be very helpful on its own. However, if this insight, or explanation, is offered to you at a time when you're free to experience the feelings that go along with it, and if this happens quite a few times, you can make the insight your own and be affected in new and transformative ways.

You might know someone who's been thoroughly "therapized." He's seen lots of shrinks, and he's able to sum himself up in a neat nutshell. He knows himself inside out; by now he has a script. So what? He's still a pain in the neck.

An important aspect of this pairing of insight and feeling in therapy is that it happens repeatedly in the context of many different conversations. One woman I treated, Rachel, had been raised by a depressed, single mother who was extremely controlling and intrusive. As a result, Rachel had an understandable difficulty allowing people to be close to her. This problem manifested itself throughout her life; her husband complained about her lack of interest in sex, her children found her emotionally distant, and Rachel herself felt sad at her lack of female friends. In therapy we were able to look at the common theme in all these relationships. Each time we looked at Rachel's current relationships and connected them to her painful experiences with her mother, we added to her understanding. Rachel rarely had huge new insights. It was more as if she were examining and reexamining the multifaceted prism of her *self*, turning it anew and seeing the light reflected and refracted in new ways.

Think of an Olympic diver. He practices the same dive, over and over, day after day. The diver listens hard to his coach's suggestions, but can't quite get it. Then one day, finally—maybe his coach finds a better metaphor, or maybe the diver is simply *ready*—he does it just right. And from then on he owns the dive, it's in his body and it's his to keep. He doesn't always get a perfect ten. Maybe now he averages a six or an eight, but that's better than the twos he used to score. And he knows how to do the dive, so when he starts to make mistakes he can get himself back on track. The point in therapy that's analogous to nailing the dive is called an *aha moment*. The process of building to that point is called "working through."

Once we're adults, our ways of being and patterns of relating are pretty well established. It's a tall order to change them. Sometimes altering entrenched aspects of our characters can feel like chipping away at concrete. Working through in therapy is the chipping away. It's what lets us reexperience and rework our important relationships, and develop new ways of relating to our inner and outer worlds. In working through we encounter, sift, reorder, rehash, digest, and metabolize our experiences. And it can often feel like slow, hard work. But it's the working through, more than the lightning flashes of insight, that is the substance of psychodynamic therapy.

THE BASICS OF PSYCHODYNAMIC THERAPY

- It is a collaborative partnership between you and your therapist.
- It has at its heart a special therapeutic relationship characterized by a frame, an approach, trust, nonjudgmental listening, caring, empathy, and a good fit.
- Within this therapeutic relationship, you should feel safe to discuss the problems that brought you to therapy and the feelings associated with them.
- The therapist will guide you toward making connections between feelings and experiences in the past and feelings and experiences in the present.
- Understanding and growth will come out of repeatedly experiencing old emotions in the new therapeutic setting, and pairing them with new intellectual understandings.

So you can see that psychodynamic therapy, unlike cognitive/behavioral therapy, isn't prescriptive. It's a collaborative process. Yes, your psychodynamic therapist should be an expert in your problem area. She should have a way of understanding you that's new and different from yours, and should be able to help you develop new insights about yourself. But therapists can't read minds. Our good understanding of you is based on your being as open and honest as you can. When it's hard for you to be open and honest, you should be prepared to explore why.

Don't despair if you don't feel, at this moment, much like running right out and hiring a therapist. All of this may seem complicated or technical. Actually, when you're in therapy, you won't think much about how it works. Even if therapy is hard at times, because it deals with hard topics, it will soon come to feel natural. Once you get used to your therapist, you'll become absorbed in the relationship and the process. Therapy is really just you and a well-trained person who cares about you working together to understand you better. And, in the end, what will really help you to get a handle on your problems is the feeling that you are profoundly understood.

PART THREE

Taking the Leap

SIX

Getting Ready to Shop

BEFORE YOU START the process of looking for a therapist, it'll be helpful to ask yourself some beginning questions. This will help you narrow your options, and make it easier to assess whether a practitioner is right for you. If you're unclear about some or all of the answers to these questions, don't worry.

What Problems Do I Want Help With?

It's often difficult to say what we want help with. Even if there's a specific event that precipitates our decision to go into therapy (say, trouble in a loving partnership or the death of a loved one), the issues involved are probably more general (say, depression, anxiety, or unstable patterns of relationships). Unless you have a specific issue you want to work on in a focused way that requires specialized training (we discussed these issues in Chapter Three), it's not necessary to seek out a specialist.

What Can I afford to Pay, and Will My Insurance Help?

For many of us, money worry is the biggest obstacle to getting the help we need. One of the most important reasons I wrote this book is to let you know there are amazing therapy bargains out there. You'll learn about those in Chapter Seven.

Therapy fees vary greatly, by the therapist's setting (private practice versus clinic), by the therapist's experience, and by geographical region. Generally speaking, psychiatrists charge the most, followed by psychologists, social workers, psychiatric nurses, licensed marriage and family therapists, and certified counselors. However, there are many exceptions. A higher fee doesn't necessarily indicate a better therapist, and a lower fee doesn't necessarily indicate a bargain.

Now let's look at insurance options:

Health Maintenance Organizations (HMOs) and Preferred Provider Organizations (PPOs)

Many people are baffled by the question of whether or not their insurance will cover therapy, and, if it does, whether they should use an in-network or out-of-network therapist, or a therapist recommended by their HMO. Let's start by considering PPO plans. These are insurance plans that give you the option of seeing a therapist on their list of participating providers. You pay the therapist a small copayment, and the therapist bills the insurance company directly for the balance of the fee. These plans usually give you another option of seeing an out-of-network provider. If you opt to go out of the network, you'll have to pay the therapist directly and file the claims yourself. Reimbursement rates for out-of-network therapists are lower. That is, you'll have to pay more. For most people, the temptation is to go with the first option, staying within the network and seeing a therapist for little or no out-of-pocket cost. It sounds like a good deal and it sometimes is, but appearances can be deceiving.

Most insurance plans cap out either at a maximum number of sessions per year (say, twenty), or at a dollar amount per calendar year. If you seek treatment from someone who participates in your plan, you're initially only responsible for a copayment, which could be a low flat fee (about ten to twenty-five dollars per session) or could be the difference between the amount of the approved charges for the services provided and the amount the company actually pays the therapist.

Let's say that you do opt to go into treatment with someone who participates with your insurance company. For a while the treatment won't cost you much, but within a couple of months you'll probably have exhausted your benefits. At that point, the only way you'll be able to continue with this therapist is by paying the full fee out of pocket.

If you go the other route and opt for an out-of-network provider, insurance will typically pay a fairly large percentage of the therapist's fee for, say, the first twenty sessions, and then some lower percentage after that until you reach your maximum. What I've found is that, with rare exceptions, the actual dollar difference between in- and out-of-network reimbursements over the course of a year ends up being negligible. More importantly, if you opt to stay out of network you'll have many more therapists to choose from.

Note that insurance companies often interfere in the course of therapy. They do this by making ongoing coverage contingent on your therapist's being able to demonstrate that your treatment is progressing in a way that satisfies their claims adjuster. Your therapist may be asked to submit periodic "treatment summaries" describing details of her work with you. So much for confidentiality! The company will review the information to assess whether it feels you need more therapy or not. Even if the company agrees you need to continue, you'll have to live with the looming prospect of the next review. Meddling by insurance companies is invasive and a pain in the neck. Most well-trained therapists agree that it has nothing to do with your best interest.

If you have medical insurance, you should start your search for a therapist by calling the company to clarify exactly what mental health services they will cover and for how long. Reimbursement rates will vary by discipline in proportion to the actual fees charged. To get a clear sense of what your out-of-pocket expenses will be, you'll have to ask specific questions about reimbursement rates for specific services provided by specific types of therapists. The problem is that insurance companies reimburse not for what the therapist actually charges, but for what the company considers to be an acceptable "reasonable and customary charge" for a given service. If you ask them what they consider to be a "customary charge" for therapy, they'll usually say they can't tell you without a "procedure code" for the exact service you'll be getting. This is because they don't want to tip you off about which services receive the highest reimbursement. They figure that if they keep you in the dark you might seek a cheaper service. It's a Catch-22: until you've had the treatment and received a bill you don't know what the procedure code is, but you can't figure out whether or not you can afford the treatment without the code.

Don't panic. It's likely nobody has told you before now that there's a simple solution to this problem. Like all health-care providers, therapists bill insurance companies by assigning a procedure code to the treatment they've provided. This code comes from the *Manual of Current Procedural Terminology* (CPT). I'm not allowed to publish the codes here, but all therapists have to know them. You can buy the manual yourself, but it's expensive. A better idea is to call a potential therapist, tell her you're interested in exploring the idea of therapy with her, and ask for the procedure code of the service you're interested in (say, individual psychotherapy or couple therapy) so you can run it by your insurance company. The potential therapist will tell you the code, and then you can call your insurance company and ask about reimbursement rates.

Now let's consider that notorious institution, the HMO. If you're covered by an HMO, then in order for your mental health care to be covered by your policy, you'll have to go to someone on their approved provider list. The advantage is that there will be little or no cost to you; the disadvantage is that your choices will be limited, as will the number of sessions covered by your plan. Once you've completed your prescribed course of treatment (usually six to twelve sessions), you'll have to quit or transfer to a different therapist outside your plan and pay the fee yourself.

Insurance isn't always such a bargain once you take into account your deductible, low rates of reimbursement, the fact that your benefits are likely to cap out before your treatment is complete, the hassle of paperwork, and the possibility that the company might interfere in your treatment. Many good therapists don't participate with insurance plans because they resent the paperwork (which introduces a significant cost of doing business to them) and, even more, the control over the length and quality of treatment that insurance companies impose. Instead, a lot us have decided to adopt a sliding scale fee, or to allocate a portion of our therapy hours to patients who need a fee reduction. We don't advertise this aspect of our practices because, let's face it, no good businessperson would lead by saying you could pay less for his service than the asking price. But if a particular therapist's stated fee is a stretch, you should always ask if there's any flexibility. The worst thing that could happen is that you're told "no." Don't simply assume you can't afford a particular therapist because he doesn't participate in your plan.

By the way, I always tell my patients that, while I don't participate with any plans, I'll happily do whatever I can to help them get reimbursed. This includes filling out their insurance forms if necessary. Some therapists will balk at this (a very few will even charge for the extra time), but most have accepted paperwork as part of life.

Do I Want Individual, Couple, Family, or Group Therapy?

Most people want individual therapy. However, if you and your life partner or other family members have identified your problem as shared, then you'll want to begin by asking any potential therapists if they work with couples and/or families. Sometimes what begins as individual therapy work expands, either by bringing family members into sessions with your therapist, or by your therapist referring them to another practitioner with whom they can collaborate. So if you think that's a possibility, it's a good idea to ask potential clinicians what kinds of therapy they practice besides individual, or if they're comfortable collaborating with other professionals.

Group therapy is another matter. If you know that you want group therapy, either because your individual therapist has suggested it or because you've decided on your own to give it a try, you'll have to do some research. Some private practitioners run groups, but most groups are run by clinics and training institutions. You can look for group therapists the same way that you do any other kind, or by calling the American Group Psychotherapy Association for referral suggestions (consult the Resources section for contact information).

Do I Want to Consider Taking Psychiatric Medications?

If you're already on medication or know you want to try it, you might consider interviewing psychiatrists exclusively. After all, they're the only mental health professionals who can prescribe medications. If you're interested in doing talk therapy at the same time, be sure to ask the psychiatrist if she provides that as well. Some do, but many don't. I've seen lots of patients who had first been to a psychiatrist and found themselves prescribed a drug and sent away after only fifteen or thirty minutes.

If you're considering a therapist who isn't a psychiatrist and think you might be a candidate for medication, ask him if he's comfortable collaborating with a psychiatrist and can recommend a good one. It's the responsibility of a therapist of any discipline to recommend that you be evaluated by a psychiatrist if they feel you need it.

Am I Looking for Any Special Demographics in a Therapist?

You may want to see someone who shares something important with you. For example, if you're gay you might want to see a gay therapist. If you're an immigrant you may feel a therapist of immigrant extraction can best understand your experience. You may have particular preferences for the age, gender, race, or religion of your therapist. So, should you set out to find a therapist who has the particular characteristics with which you are most concerned?

Well, if you're disabled, you could make a good argument that a similarly disabled therapist could best understand your experience. On the other hand, the fact that he's disabled doesn't necessarily make him a good listener or good at understanding your other issues. It also doesn't guarantee he's well trained.

This is what I think. Issues of difference come up all the time, in therapy as in life. No matter how hard you try to find a therapist like you, in the end you're the only one like you. A therapist shouldn't assume he understands you just because he shares one or more of your characteristics. A patient of mine, a Korean-American woman, recently complained about an experience she had with her former therapist: "He kept saying he understood me because his wife is Korean and he knows all about the problems of Korean families. He decided what I was all about before we even started. He didn't really want to get to know me."

We all have to guard against making assumptions about people based on their superficial similarities to and differences from us; therapists are not immune to this failing. But good therapists try to meet each new patient on the patient's own terms, with fresh eyes and ears. You can tell your therapist about cultural issues; she'll be interested in learning about these and about things that make you unique. But what determines a good match between you and your therapist is not the superficial similarity between you, but the depth of understanding that grows between you over time.

Do I Have an Initial Preference for Short- versus Long-Term Therapy?

Let's face it, most of us don't go into therapy hoping it will take a long time. Some people find the idea of open-ended therapy overwhelming and would prefer to work for a shorter time on specific goals.

Most therapists, even those who don't particularly specialize in short-term treatment, will happily "contract" with you for a set number of sessions, with the goal of resolving a specific problem. Before you go into short-term therapy, though, be sure to clarify what will happen at the end of the "contract." If you haven't reached your goal but feel you're making progress, or if you've identified a new goal, most therapists will offer you the option of signing on for more sessions. A few will insist on stopping anyway; so check ahead.

Is My Schedule Unpredictable?

There are many life circumstances that might make it hard for you to commit to regular appointments. Maybe you have a job with an unpredictable schedule, or have children with someone who does. Maybe you have health problems that sporadically incapacitate you, or have an ill family member who requires you to stay home from time to time. Don't let a fluctuating schedule keep you away.

If you openly discuss scheduling concerns, you'll find that most therapists will work out a feasible plan. Some will schedule appointments week by week, rather than asking you to commit to a regular time, and others will conduct telephone sessions when you can't make it in. I even have colleagues who conduct ongoing marriage therapy when one spouse travels a lot; they just plan some sessions as conference calls.

If you're likely to need special arrangements, be sure to bring the issue up early on. Some therapists are more flexible than others.

Will Getting to the Nearest Well-trained Therapist on a Regular Basis Be Difficult?

If you live in the country or some other remote setting, don't assume you can't find an excellent therapist. Many have developed methods for effectively and ethically treating people who live too far away to come in to their offices on a regular basis. The protocol in such cases typically involves a combination of face-to-face sessions (say once or twice per month) and telephone sessions. Some therapists even do video sessions over DSL lines with computers, but this is still new and developing in the field. You must always meet your therapist in person before you start working with him. This will ensure that he is who he says, and will set the stage for a real (not a virtual) therapeutic relationship.

Do I Have a Preference for a Therapist with a Particular Kind of Training?

While a therapist's degree tells you very little about their clinical expertise, their post-degree training and hands-on experience are critical in determining if a particular clinician is right for you (refer back to Chapter Three for a full discussion).

SEVEN

Shopping

SO YOU'VE DECIDED to consult a therapist. Believe it or not, you've already done the hard part. Once you've made the mental shift toward being open to the idea of psychotherapy, the rest of the search is just shopping. And I don't mean an exhausting day at a five-hundred-store outlet center. This might sound strange to you, but shopping for a therapist should be interesting. It should also be a relief, because you're now going to do something about your problem.

Think of the way you feel when you decide to buy something you've wanted for a long time. Say it's a car. For a while you grumble about your old one. It's unreliable, uncomfortable, and decidedly uncool. But you have other financial priorities, so you live with it. Then one day you're late for work and the darn thing won't start. You realize that no matter what your other financial commitments are, you have to buy a new car.

Now you're excited, because you've lived with this need for long enough that you feel deserving, not guilty. So you look through some car magazines, surf the Web, and test-drive a few models.

You're not going to obsess, but you're going to gather enough information that when you make your purchase you'll feel you've given yourself a present.

I want you to feel that way now. Relax: you are the consumer, and the therapists out there have a service to offer. While it's important to comparison-shop, it's not necessary to get bogged down in the feeling that you have to follow every lead, or interview dozens of potential therapists for fear of not finding the perfect match. Just be prepared to use the same judgment you'd use when buying your new car—a combination of research, preference, and intuition.

> **Relax: you are the consumer, and the therapists out there have a service to offer. While it's important to comparison-shop, it's not necessary to get bogged down in the feeling that you have to follow every lead, or interview dozens of potential therapists for fear of not finding the perfect match. Just be prepared to use the same judgment you'd use when buying your new car— a combination of research, preference, and intuition.**

As a general rule, I recommend you interview at least two, maybe even three, people before making a decision. There are exceptions; on your first try you might meet someone who's a fantastic fit for you. That's fine; go for it. But, especially if this is your first time in therapy, you won't have any point of reference for making your decision until you can compare the way you feel with therapists of differing styles and personalities.

Let's consider, one at a time, specific referral sources.

Word of Mouth

This is the most popular way of finding a therapist, and it's not a bad one. If someone you trust recommends a clinician she's seen and liked, that recommendation could be worth a lot. But when it comes to therapy, one size definitely does not fit all. If your friend (or hairdresser, or colleague) recommends her therapist, by all means schedule an appointment. But keep an open mind; you're looking for a good match for you.

Also, think carefully before working with a practitioner who is treating someone you know well. There are no hard and fast rules on this; therapists tend to develop their own policies. For example, I generally don't treat close friends or family members of current patients, but I know many therapists who do. But ask yourself: how would sharing the same therapist with a good friend affect your friendship and your therapy? Would you worry about what your friend was saying about you in their sessions? Would you worry that your therapist liked your friend better, or gave more weight to her version of events? Would you worry that your therapist talked about you with your friend? These are all issues that could be discussed and potentially worked through. On the other hand, I think therapy works best when the boundaries between it and your outside life are as clean as possible (see Chapter Nine).

Your Physician

Medical doctors can be good sources of referrals, but not all of them are as supportive of or as knowledgeable about therapy as others. And their referral roster may be short if they have only collaborated with a few therapists. Sometimes, but not always, physicians prefer to refer to psychiatrists, who are also medical doctors. Again, be sure that any psychiatrist you are referred to is a therapist, not just someone who prescribes medication.

Your Insurance Company

If you decide you want to use your plan, there is a simple way of narrowing the field. Call someone you trust, say your physician or a therapist that a friend says is great, and ask if she'd be willing to take a look at the list of providers from your insurance company and let you know whom she'd recommend from the list. I perform this service all the time, both for people I've never met and for patients who are considering going into treatment with me but want to shop around a bit. I have them fax me the list, then I take a look at it and circle some possibilities, and I fax it back to them. The whole process takes me two minutes, and it helps people feel less as if they're stumbling in the dark. Remember: whether your insurance company is a PPO or an HMO, interview more than one therapist before you choose.

The Yellow Pages, Media Advertisements, and Internet Search Engines

If you live in a rural area, an advertisement or the telephone book might be the only way you have of finding a therapist. But if you live in or near even a middle-sized city, you have lots of choices. The fact that a therapist has a quarter-page ad in the telephone book, his face on the side of a bus, or his practice listed with Internet search engines says more about his entrepreneurial spirit than his clinical skills. On the other hand, business savvy and clinical savvy are not mutually exclusive. A word of caution: when your referral comes from an advertisement rather than a trusted friend or professional, it's more important than ever to comparison-shop.

Internet Sites Providing Online Psychotherapy

Believe it or not, some Internet sites will connect you to a therapist who will actually conduct your entire therapy online, either by e-mail or in a chat format. Many of these sites claim their therapists are fully trained and qualified, and they tout themselves as offering therapy without the inconvenience of leaving home. They suggest that online therapy is good for everyone and the treatment of choice for the disabled and people who are afraid to leave home (agoraphobics).

Online therapy is the kind of bizarre practice that leaves most of us shaking our heads. The problems with it are so fundamental that if a therapist doesn't see them, he shouldn't be in practice in the first place. First, there is no assurance of confidentiality on the Internet. Even if communications are encrypted, they can sometimes be broken into. Also, how do you know who's reading your messages on the other end? Second, there is no way to be sure that the person you're communicating with is the person she claims to be. Even if the therapist sends you a copy of her license, how do you know she's the person providing the service? Finally, you can't do therapy by passing notes back and forth. Typing is too slow for communicating the fullness and spontaneity of thoughts. Besides, a large part of what therapists do is pay attention to nonverbal communications such as silences, tones of voice, eye contact, body movements, and postures. These are all equally as important as words, and can't be conveyed online.

I don't say it often, but I'll say it here: Don't do this. It isn't therapy.

College Clinics and Employee Assistance Programs (EAPs)

If you're a college student or someone who works for a large company, chances are you have access to some free mental health services. But like HMOs, neither college nor EAP clinics provide long-term services. If you go to one of these, you'll probably be seen for six to twelve sessions, at the end of which you'll either have to stop treatment or accept a referral to an outside therapist. College and EAP clinics can be good places to go for help in a crisis or for a referral for longer-term treatment. If you're not sure if these services are available to you, the best place to start for colleges/universities is typically the school's health center, and for EAP programs your company's human resources department, if you have one.

Community Mental Health Clinics

Community mental health clinics can be great places to get lower-cost therapy. These clinics are not-for-profit, and are often part of larger agencies that may be partially funded by private foundations or state departments of mental health. Some are housed in agencies that have religious affiliations. For example, where I work in the Washington, D.C., area, we have Jewish Social Service, Family and Child Services,

Catholic Charities, and several others. Don't be put off if you're not religious or are of another faith; most of these agencies have diverse staffs and are committed to serving the entire community. Also, many universities have treatment clinics, staffed by advanced trainees, which offer low-cost therapy to the public. If you have any question about a particular clinic, call them to clarify their mission.

The quality of treatment provided in community clinics varies widely. I would recommend asking around a bit to get a sense of a particular clinic's reputation. Therapy in these clinics is usually provided by clinical social workers or graduate students in social work, under the supervision of a licensed social worker, certified counselor, or licensed marriage and family therapist. The staff usually includes at least one psychologist who may do therapy but is available to do diagnostic testing, and a consultant psychiatrist for medications. There is usually a range of experience among the staff, but there's no reason you can't request one of the more senior therapists.

Community mental heath clinics can be wonderful resources if you have a physical disability; unlike private practices, they are required to be wheelchair accessible. Also, clinics are good places to look if English isn't your first language, as many offer treatment in multiple languages.

> **Community mental heath clinics can be wonderful resources if you have a physical disability; unlike private practices, they are required to be wheelchair accessible. Also, clinics are good places to look if English isn't your first language, as many offer treatment in multiple languages.**

It can be hard to find these clinics in the telephone book, since they are as likely to be listed by name as by the specific services that they offer. The best way to find them is by looking in the yellow pages under headings such as "therapy" or "psychotherapy." Another way to find them is to call your state's department of mental health for a listing of local non-profit agencies offering mental health services.

Hospital Outpatient Mental Health Clinics

Many hospitals with psychiatry departments and virtually all psychiatric hospitals have outpatient clinics. These clinics primarily, though not exclusively, treat former inpatients and other patients of the doctors who work at the hospital. As a result, the clientele of these clinics tends to have relatively severe emotional problems. Also, these clinics tend to emphasize the medical treatment of psychiatric illness and the psychological issues associated with medical illness.

Addiction, Detoxification, and 12-Step Programs

Most therapists, whether in private practice or a clinic, will refuse to treat someone with a substance abuse problem unless he's also enrolled in or has completed a treatment program specifically designed to treat the addiction.

These programs are not difficult to find in the Yellow Pages, and you'll see many of them in the Resources section of this book. You can also call your local hospital. It will either have a program in-house, or will be able to direct you to the right place.

And finally, drum roll please. . . .

The Best Unsung Sources of Therapy Bargains in the World: Therapy and Psychoanalysis Training Programs

There are thousands of schools in this country dedicated to the training of mental health clinicians. They are usually not called schools, but "institutes," "societies," or "centers." Regardless, their students, or "trainees," are mental health practitioners who have already qualified to practice. In fact, many have already done therapy for years and now want to deepen their knowledge of a particular type of treatment or theoretical orientation. Note: trainees in therapy training programs are honing their skills in therapy, while trainees in psychoanalysis are already well-trained therapists who are going on to specialize in psychoanalysis.

Both therapy and psychoanalysis training programs typically require trainees to take classes in theory and technique, undergo their own personal therapy or psychoanalysis, and treat patients under the supervision of a teacher who is a senior clinician. This means that the trainee, your therapist, is required to meet on a regular basis with someone with many more years of experience to discuss the progress of her cases. The happy result is that patients in her care get thought about a lot, by two good minds. These discussions are governed by the same confidentiality rules as is therapy (see Chapter Nine).

Even though, or perhaps because, therapists in these institutes are in the process of honing their skills, they typically provide some of the most thoughtful and sensitive treatment available. Although it's been many years since my first institute training, I still remember vivid details about the patients I worked with under supervision. You should know that therapists don't come out of their training programs with new credentials, and they won't be entitled to charge more for their services. Their motivation for entering these programs is simply to be better therapists. That means trainees tend to be a particularly dedicated and thoughtful group.

Here's the exciting part. Most of these training programs have clinics (often called treatment centers) attached to them. In these clinics, trainees (remember, these are well-qualified clinicians) provide therapy for a sliding scale fee based on income. Many will accept insurance, but all are dedicated to providing high-quality, affordable treatment to their communities. Depending on how a particular clinic is structured, therapy might be conducted at the clinic itself or in the therapists' private offices.

But if you want to make profound, substantive changes in your life, you should consider this: psychoanalysis from a trainee is by far the most therapy you will get for your buck. If you go into analysis with a trainee, you'll be seen three or more times per week for very little money, sometimes as little as ten to twenty dollars per session. Psychoanalysts in training dedicate enormous time and energy to their work. Think about it: you'd be getting excellent, intensive help from an experienced clinician several times per week (most likely in a private office) for less than it would cost to see someone else once a week. If your interest is piqued, go back and reread my description of psychoanalysis in Chapter Three.

Remember, whether it's psychoanalysis or therapy you want, or if you're unsure, you can (and should) call more than one institution to set up consultations. Even training institutions that don't have their own formal clinics encourage the public to call for referrals to their trainees.

You may be wondering why, if these institutes offer such great therapy bargains, you haven't heard about them? Well, as I said in the Introduction, we therapists are terrible at advertising what we offer. Unfortunately, there's no Great List, no central source of information on institutions offering low-fee therapy with trainees. But unless you live in a rural setting, you're likely to be within reasonable distance of several. One of the main reasons I wrote this book was to let you know that these places exist, and that they can make good therapy available to people who couldn't afford it otherwise. If you're interested in therapy but have limited financial resources, I recommend doing a little research into institutes. It'll be well worth your time

TIPS FOR FINDING GOOD LOW-FEE THERAPY OR PSYCHOANALYSIS

THE TRICK is in locating the institutes (therapist training schools) near you that offer low-fee therapy with their trainees (therapists in training). It's really not hard. Here are some suggestions:

- Since many institutes are not affiliated with any national group, the easiest and best way to find them is to ask a therapist that you (or someone you trust) likes. Established mental health professionals in your community should know the names of the local training institutes, and which ones have solid reputations. They'll also be likely to know which training institutes have which theoretical orientations.

- Try the Web: plug in keywords "psychotherapy" (or "psychoanalysis," if that's what you want), "training," and the name of your state or community. Other keyword possibilities: "institute," "low-cost therapy (or psychotherapy)," "counseling," "sliding scale."

- There's always the telephone book. Look under the headings Therapy, Psychotherapy, Counseling, and Mental Health. If you're looking specifically for couple, marriage, or family therapy, try those headings, too. If you see a listing and you're not sure what services they offer, just call and ask if they are a training institute. If they are, ask if they have a clinic or can offer a referral to a trainee, and what their fee range is.

- Many professional organizations maintain regional lists of training institutes that focus on specific modalities. You might try one (or a few) of the following if it suits your interests. You'll find the contact information in the Resources section of this book:

     American Association of Marriage and Family Therapists
     American Association of Sex Educators, Counselors, and
          Therapists
     American Family Therapy Academy
     American Group Psychotherapy Association

- Some institutes have loose or formal affiliations to professional associations. There are probably hundreds of such associations, but I've listed several of the better-known ones below. Again, you'll find contact information in the Resources section:

     Association for Autonomous Psychoanalytic Institutes
     American Psychoanalytic Association
     American Psychological Association Division of
          Psychoanalysis (Division 39), Section of Psychologist
          Psychoanalytic Practitioners (Section 1)
     Council of Psychoanalytic Psychotherapists
     National Association for the Advancement of Psychoanalysis
     National Social Work Federation's National Membership
          Committee on Psychoanalysis in Clinical Social Work

EIGHT

The Initial Consultation

ONCE YOU'VE GATHERED a few telephone numbers, it's time to set a first consultation. This is a mutual interview, a chance for you and the therapist to decide if there's a good fit between you. The process can take anywhere from one to several sessions. You should never jump right into treatment with someone new. There are a number of things you need to know about each other first. Some of the information you'll gather will be factual, and some of it will be intuitive—but all of it will be informative. Let's go over the important aspects of a therapy consultation, so you'll know what to expect.

The First Telephone Call

For most people, this is the hardest part. So if you've put off making this call, or if you're anxious about it, you're not alone. Actually, most therapists don't like to get into lengthy discussions before meeting someone in person. They'd prefer to briefly cover a few key points, and then, still on the phone, decide with you whether to set up an appointment. Understandably, busy professionals don't want to waste a lot of phone time speaking to someone they're not yet working with, and anyway it's much better to get into meatier issues face to face.

Calling a Clinic

Unlike private practices, clinics often have receptionists who answer the phone. If so, you should identify yourself as someone who's interested in therapy and ask to speak with the "intake worker." This is a therapist whose job is to schedule appointments for new patients, and it may or may not be the person with whom you'll actually meet for the consultation.

Intake workers are likely to ask the usual identifying questions (name, address, phone number), as well as the type of insurance you have, if any. They'll also ask the nature of the problem, and may even discuss it with you in some detail. They'll do this is order to determine if the kinds of services they offer are appropriate for you, and which of their therapists might be a good match.

Once you have an appointment set up, be sure to ask about the background and qualifications of the therapist who'll be conducting the interview, and whether or not that therapist would be continuing with you beyond the consultation. It's common in clinics for one therapist to do what is called an "assessment" (one or more meetings with a new patient to determine the nature of the problems and decide on a treatment plan), and then transfer the case to another staff member. Also, be sure to ask about fees, and whether or not you'll be placed on a waiting list for therapy, either before or after the consultation. If you are placed on a waiting list, be sure to ask how long you'll have to wait. And then keep calling back to check on your status. Though some clinics (especially the really good ones) often have months-long waiting lists, the squeaky wheel often gets assigned to a therapist first.

Calling a Private Practice

Since therapists can't be interrupted while they're working, they're hard to reach. You might increase your chances if you call just before the top of the hour, but even so, you're likely to get an answering machine. Leave your name (it's okay not to leave your last name if you don't want to, but your message will be confidential) and telephone number, say who (if anyone) referred you, and that you would like to talk about scheduling a consultation appointment. That's it—you don't need to go into more detail. You can reasonably expect to receive a call back within twenty-four to forty-eight hours. If it takes longer, move to the next therapist on your list. You want someone responsive, not someone who makes you wait days for a return call. And the therapist should call you in person. If you get a call back from a receptionist or secretary, that's usually a bad sign. You want someone who believes in the personal touch. Unless there's a good explanation (such as the therapist being out of town), opt for someone else.

When the therapist does call back, briefly describe your problem ("I've been feeling depressed, and am interested in getting help," or "My wife and I would like someone to talk to about our marriage"). You may feel pressure to go into more detail. That's normal; you're finally talking to someone who might be able to help, and you have a lot to say. Plus, you want to be sure this therapist is really the right one. But you really can't determine that at this stage. Even if you view your problem as specific or convoluted, it's not necessary to go into a lot of detail over the phone.

Simply ask the therapist if he has time for new patients, and if he'd be willing to meet with you for a consultation. If he says "yes," ask him to tell you something about himself—remember the "Five Categories" (see Chapter Three): What is his degree in and theoretical orientation? Does he have experience in the particular modality (individual, couple, family, and the like) you want? And if you're looking for a therapist with expertise in a particular technique (such as EMDR) or specialty area (such as eating disorders), does he have experience in it? You're entitled to answers to these questions, and if the therapist acts put off or defensive, or says he'll only answer them in person (that is, on the clock)—forget it.

If fees are a concern, you should ask about them in this first phone call. How much does the therapist charge, and does she accept insurance? If you think her fee is more than you can afford but you've heard she's really good, consider seeing her for a consultation anyway. It can be worthwhile to see an experienced and skilled clinician, even if it's only for a session or two, to help you organize your thoughts about your problem and formulate a good plan for getting help. Once she knows you, this therapist will be able to make just the right referral to someone else you *can* afford. Also, many therapists will consider reducing their fee once they've gotten to know you, if they sense they're really the best person to help you, you're highly motivated to work in therapy, and you really need the reduction. The more flexible you can be about appointment times the more likely you are to get a lower fee, since many therapists have certain hours that are hard to fill.

Finally, if you have a tight schedule (for example, if you can only see a therapist in the early morning or on the weekends), ask in that first call if she'll be able to accommodate you. If not, keep in mind that therapist's schedules shift around as patients request time changes or leave. Sometimes it's worth starting with someone you really like even at an inconvenient time, if that'll put you in line for a better time when it becomes available. If you do find yourself stuck with an inconvenient time, be sure your therapist knows that you want to be kept in mind for when a better time becomes available.

The First Meeting

You're bound to be nervous. What will he be like? Will he embarrass you or make you feel stupid? Will he be able to help? Did you make a mistake by coming? Therapists handle the first meeting in different ways. Let's look at some possibilities.

The Setting

First, you'll scan the environment for clues about what's coming. If you're going to a clinic or hospital, the environment is bound to feel a bit sterile and institutional. You'll be looking around at the other patients in the waiting room ("Are they like me?"), and getting an impression of the place by the way the administrative staff treats you. Is there a friendly receptionist? Does the place feel organized and professionally run? Is the furniture comfortable and clean? You won't be able to help being influenced by these factors, but try not to worry about them too much. If you're lucky enough to get a wonderful therapist, the trappings won't matter after a while. On the other hand, if you're treated disrespectfully by any member of the clinic staff, or if you feel that your confidentiality isn't protected (no employee should discuss patients or use patients' names outside of a private office), go elsewhere.

Therapists in private practice work in lots of different places, ranging from office buildings to private homes. They sometimes work alone (solo practice), and sometimes in groups. A few have secretaries or receptionists, but most don't. Regardless, don't get too wrapped up in judging the decor. Some therapists spend a lot of money on office furniture, while others go for thrift-store chic. Some therapists rent furnished space on either a full- or part-time basis—so you can't learn much about them from aesthetics. None of this has any bearing on the quality of a clinician's work. What's important is that the space be accessible and professionally organized, and that the office itself be soundproofed. Don't be surprised if the office has two doors on the same frame, since that's often the only way of completing the soundproofing.

The Interview

A therapist should begin a consultation interview by asking you to say a bit about yourself and what brought you. This is your chance to describe your problem, or how you're feeling, in whatever way you want. You shouldn't feel pressured to include all the details of your situation or your history. Just say whatever's on your mind, and don't try too hard to sort it all out. It took you a long time to get to this point, maybe years, and no therapist can know you well in forty-five or fifty minutes. You don't have to cram everything you want her to know into one session; it's fine if you need more time to tell your story.

At this point the therapist should be listening attentively, and perhaps asking a few clarifying questions. She shouldn't jump in with

premature interpretations, nor repeatedly interrup
subject. As a psychodynamic therapist (see Chapt
I don't like to direct these sessions too much. I
"history" of new patients. I'm interested in th
course, and whatever may have happened to them
tributing to problems now. But the best way for
know you is to listen to your story as *you* tell it
important feelings and themes as they unfold.

If you're being seen by a clinic intake worker, she may ask you a series of questions. She'll probably have to make a rapid assessment, so she'll have to get a lot of information quickly. A cognitive/behavioral therapist might also conduct a structured interview, as that therapy is highly structured and problem-focused.

Regardless of the setting, the theoretical orientation of the clinician, or the structure of the interview, you should experience the therapist as warm, empathic, respectful, and interested in understanding you and your problem. You should:

- Sense that the therapist is thoughtful and intelligent
- Not feel pushed to explain yourself too quickly
- Not feel the therapist is making snap judgments about you
- Not feel pressured into answering questions you don't want to answer or revealing things about yourself you prefer to keep private for now

A good therapist will be able to pull together the symptoms you describe, the history you share, and most important, the way you feel about them and interact with them, in order to paint a coherent picture. What's going on in the room between you and the therapist is more important than anything else, because it's alive and available for both of you to look at together. For example, if you consult a therapist because you feel depressed, the therapist might at some point offer: "Well, it does sound as though you've been having an awfully hard time. You describe that you've been sleeping a lot, and you don't feel much like working or spending time with friends. And here, today, I've noticed that you're critical of yourself and don't really like to look me

e. I'm wondering about that." Opening up an emotional
e" for the two of you to look at what's happening between you
the quickest and best way to arrive at a real understanding of your
problem, rather than a pat, quick, or intellectual one.

> **A good therapist will be able to pull together the
> symptoms you describe, the history you share, and most
> important, the way you feel about them and interact
> with them, in order to paint a coherent picture. What's
> going on in the room between you and the therapist is
> more important than anything else, because it's alive and
> available for both of you to look at together.**

Once you have explained your problem, how should the therapist
respond? Unless you've been given something to hold on to, you
won't want to come back. You'll need a reason; that's only natural.
Even in a one- or two-session consultation, a good therapist will be
able to give you the flavor of how she works, so you'll know what
therapy with her would be like. She'll also share how she sees your
problem, whether or not she agrees with your understanding of it,
and what kind of therapy she thinks you need. A clinician may say
he doesn't yet understand some important things about you, and may
suggest extending the consultation by one or more sessions. That's
okay. But you should leave even your initial meeting with at least a
feeling of hope.

> **Unless you've been given something to hold on to, you
> won't want to come back. You'll need a reason; that's
> only natural. Even in a one- or two-session consultation,
> a good therapist will be able to give you the flavor of
> how she works, so you'll know what therapy with her
> would be like.**

For example, the therapist you consult for depression might offer: "The symptoms you describe—the over-sleeping, the loss of interest in things you used to enjoy, the sadness—all certainly suggest you're depressed. And we've been talking about how you felt ashamed and worried I would judge you, just as your father did when you were a child. Even though you've lost your job, and that seems to have pushed you over the edge, it sounds as if this current crisis has brought to the surface feelings you've had for a long time. You've been feeling sad and down on yourself for years, with lots of worries about how people in authority judge you. Since your problem has been going on for a long time and is connected to your early experiences, I don't think a brief treatment will get you the kind of long-term relief you want. You'll have to decide if you're comfortable with an open-ended therapy. Since you're feeling so awful and so desperate for relief, I'd suggest meeting twice a week, at least for now. But you'll have to decide about that, too."

Ending the Session

Finally, there are practicalities to be considered. At some point during the interview, the therapist should explain the nuts and bolts of his practice. Many practitioners leave time for this at the end of the session. Even if yours doesn't, you should make sure to get your basic questions answered, such as, "What's your fee?" and "What's your cancellation policy?" If you think access to your therapist between sessions will be an issue, ask about her telephone and emergency policies.

Most therapists will end by asking if you'd like to schedule another appointment. If you're sure you want to, go ahead. But it's also fine to say you'd prefer not to, or (even if you like the therapist) to say you'd like to go home and think about it. It can be useful to let things "stew" a bit before deciding. Particularly if you're consulting a therapist for couple or family therapy, you may want to go home and discuss things with your partner in private. There's nothing wrong with telling the therapist you're shopping around; a good therapist will support the idea.

Making a Choice

Once you've interviewed two or three therapists or feel you've made a good connection with someone, how do you decide? Here are some suggestions:

Pick Someone Smart, but Not Too Intellectual

Naturally, you want someone who's intelligent, insightful, and articulate. As a patient, you should feel you're in the presence of a good mind. But in choosing a therapist you should be respectful and aware of the important tension between a good therapist's capacity to formulate an understanding of you and his willingness to suspend judgment. The ability to tolerate and work with this tension—that is, to develop working hypotheses about you that are flexible, not fixed—is at the core of good treatment. Steer clear of clinicians who (like Dr. Phil) are too quick to tell you all about yourself. No therapist can "get you" right away; quick summations are superficial at best. The therapist who presents herself as brilliant or all-knowing isn't taking the time to figure out if there's a good fit between you.

But don't you deserve the most brilliant therapist in the world? Especially if you've had therapy before (and so understand quite a lot about yourself already) or are psychologically-minded, you'll need to feel that your therapist is at least as smart (if not smarter) than you. In fact, you might consider smarts to be the most important factor in choosing a therapist. If you are concerned about your therapist's level of sophistication, then fine—I'd suggest you go with a more seasoned (less "green") professional. And do pick someone you respect. But a lot of us think we're so complicated that only the best, most brilliant therapist could possibly understand us. I should know; we therapists are particularly vulnerable to feeling this way ourselves when it's our turn to be patients. Sometimes we can use this idea to keep us from committing to therapy, or to a particular therapist. We tell ourselves, "I'm smarter than she is" or "He's not telling me anything about myself I didn't already know." Remember: therapy isn't so much about ideas as it is about feelings (see Introduction and Chapter Five). Given a basic level of professional and intellectual competence, you really need someone caring who'll *emotionally* stick by you, not just a verbal impresario.

> **A lot of us think we're so complicated that only the best, most brilliant therapist could possibly understand us.**

Pick Someone Warm, but Not Overly Charismatic

Good therapy is based on trust, not seduction. Therapists who curry hero worship or idealization succeed in keeping their patients in therapy (often for too long), but don't encourage them to become independent. At the same time, you don't want someone cold, aloof, or dull. Ask yourself: "Do I feel comfortable with this person?" Your intuition is your best guide, so go with your gut.

> **Therapists who curry hero worship or idealization succeed in keeping their patients in therapy (often for too long), but don't encourage them to become independent.**

Pick Someone Consistent, but Not Rigid

Good therapists function within a theoretical framework (see Chapter Five), but they're not captive to it. A woman who came to see me for a consultation told me the following story: After several months of trying, she finally got pregnant. She arrived at her therapist's office bursting to tell him the good news. But when she did, he didn't react at all. He just sat there in impassive silence. The woman was hurt and angry. When she asked him why he didn't congratulate her, the therapist explained that he was "waiting to see what being pregnant meant to *her*."

This anecdote illustrates how a basic tenet of therapy ("therapists should keep their own reactions in abeyance in order to make space for the patient's") can be taken to the extreme so that the therapist stops acting like a *normal person*. A good therapist isn't a "one-noter." He's flexible; he has a broad repertoire of possible ways of being. And he's *real*. If something great happens to you, he's happy; if something awful happens, he's sad. Sometimes he's warm and supportive, sometimes he pushes you or encourages you to be more introspective. Sometimes he's quiet, other times more forthcoming. From time to time, he'll laugh at your jokes—even make one. Therapy shouldn't be humorless. A good therapist will make decisions about what to say (or not say) by considering your needs at a given time, not by following a dispassionate set of rules from a therapy handbook. You want someone who has really digested the theory and science of therapy, and is therefore free to practice it as an art.

> **A good therapist will make decisions about what to say (or not say) by considering your needs at a given time, not by following a dispassionate set of rules from a therapy handbook. You want someone who has really digested the theory and science of therapy, and is therefore free to practice it as an art.**

Your Ordinary Good Judgment Applies

When we walk off the street into a therapist's office (or for that matter, into any health care provider's office), we're leaving our known world and entering someone else's, both literally and figuratively. Some people, even if they feel relief at the prospect of getting help for their problems, find the experience destabilizing. One man I know, an intelligent and successful professional who in other settings is confident, competent, and decisive, describes meeting a new therapist as being like "falling down the rabbit hole." He says: "When I go to a new therapist, I feel I'm entering their sanctuary, their inner-sanctum. I worry about falling under their 'expert' spell. I lose touch with myself and my own opinions. I hate the feeling that I've lost my capacity to make good, conscious choices."

In meeting new therapists we all reencounter aspects of ourselves. This man is describing not the qualities of the therapists he meets, but rather his own vulnerability to feeling controlled by an outside authority. That's not to say that he hasn't had the bad luck of meeting overly seductive or bossy therapists. But there's a difference between feeling controlled (or worrying about feeling controlled) and being controlled. If you have concerns about falling under the sway of a therapist's professional authority, maybe that's a fear you have in lots of settings. If so, therapy will offer the opportunity to experience, explore, and work through this fear.

But do pay attention if a therapist's manner causes you to feel *uncharacteristically* bullied, or uncomfortable in some other way. Therapy, while it has special qualities, is part of real life. Hence, your ordinary judgment applies when it comes to choosing a therapist. Good therapists want to help you develop your sense of personal agency. If you really feel a therapist is more interested in getting you to comply with her ideas and opinions than in helping you to develop your own, then maybe you're with the wrong therapist.

> **Good therapists want to help you develop your sense of personal agency. If you really feel a therapist is more interested in getting you to comply with her ideas and opinions than in helping you to develop your own, then maybe you're with the wrong therapist.**

You Don't Need a Perfect Therapist, You Need a "Good-Enough" Therapist

The psychoanalyst Donald Winnicott introduced the concept of the "good-enough mother." His idea was that children don't need perfect mothers. In fact, even if perfect mothers existed, they wouldn't *be* perfect. Every child needs a mother who meets his important needs *most* of the time, thoughtfully and with reasonable consistency. She works at understanding her child—his communications and his developmental needs—and from time to time she gets it just right. At other times she doesn't. Over the months and years, the best mother increasingly "fails," or disillusions, her child. In other words, she doesn't rush in too quickly to help or provide for the child, and she holds herself back more as he gets older and can cope better on his own. This type of good-enough parenting allows for strong emotional attachment, but also fosters autonomy and the development of the child's self-esteem (see Chapter Eleven).

The best therapists, like the best mothers, are good enough. Sometimes they get it just right—they offer an interpretation that really brings an idea into focus, or offer what feels like the perfectly comforting insight. At other times, they miss the mark. After all, they're only human. The structure of therapy has some built-in frustrations. You'll never get quite as much from your therapist, or *of* your therapist, as you want. And that's a good thing. You need a competent therapist who'll give you enough nurturing, encouragement, support, and guidance that you feel cared about and safe. But you also need one who will hold back enough that you can learn, grow, stretch, and become more independent. And although you don't get to pick your parents, you do get to pick your therapist.

> **The structure of therapy has some built-in frustrations. You'll never get quite as much from your therapist, or *of* your therapist, as you want. And that's a good thing.**

CHECKLIST FOR A
THERAPY CONSULTATION

Things to know about the therapist:

- What's his credential to practice therapy (does he have a professional degree and a license)?
- What's his theoretical orientation (psychodynamic or cognitive/behavioral)?
- What training does this therapist have in the modality (individual, couple, family, group) or special techniques (sex therapy, biofeedback) you want?
- Does this therapist have experience working with people who have problems similar to yours?
- What's her understanding of your problem?
- What treatment would this therapist recommend for you (including frequency and projected duration)?
- What are the fee and cancellation policies?
- Does she have availability that jibes with yours?
- Will the therapist be available by telephone between sessions?
- Will he be available in case of emergency?

Things to know about yourself:

- Do you feel the therapist is a competent, caring professional?
- Do you feel comfortable with the therapist?
- Do you feel the therapist has a good understanding of your problem?
- Do you feel you have a better understanding of your problem than you did before?
- Do you feel hopeful that the therapist can help?

PART FOUR

In Therapy

NINE

Ethics and Etiquette

GOING INTO THERAPY, especially for the first time, is entering unfamiliar territory. How will your therapist act? What will be expected of you? Even though therapy is practiced a bit differently by each professional, there are some general rules. This chapter is intended to familiarize you with them so you can approach treatment with a sense of what's ahead.

Besides reducing anxiety, there's another reason to know how therapy should be conducted. Like every field, this one has its bad apples. Happily, it's the exception rather than the rule, but there will always be some therapists who violate professional boundaries in dramatic or subtle ways. Sometimes the problem is the therapist's lack of skill, at other times it's bad judgment or poor moral character. But what makes unethical therapists so dangerous is how potentially influential they are to their patients. Even though you're most likely going to find yourself in the care of a competent, ethical professional, the best protection against a bad experience is education.

Ethics

Therapy isn't regulated, but most practitioners hold professional licenses and are bound by a professional code of ethics. Within this code are practice guidelines, and violating them could result in censure or loss of license, or could be the basis of a malpractice suit. The American Psychological Association has published "Principles for the Provision of Mental Health and Substance Abuse Treatment Services: A Bill of Rights," which has been officially endorsed by all the major mental health professional groups (see page 174). Unlicensed therapists aren't professionally bound by any particular code of ethics, but most will comply voluntarily because the rules make good clinical sense.

Let's go over the important principles of ethical conduct by therapists.

Confidentiality

The knowledge that what you tell your therapist will remain private is crucial. Without it, you won't feel safe to disclose your innermost thoughts and feelings.

RULES OF CONFIDENTIALITY
- With some exceptions (see below) your therapist may not discuss any aspect of your therapy with any third party without prior written consent.
- Your therapist may not even reveal that you're *in* therapy without your written consent.
- Your therapist may not release any clinical records pertaining to your treatment without such consent.
- You're free to discuss your therapy with anyone.
- Your therapist must obtain your written permission before video- or audio-taping your sessions, and must disclose under what conditions and in what ways those tapes will be used.

EXCEPTIONS TO RULES OF CONFIDENTIALITY

- Therapists are legally bound to alert the authorities if they have information suggesting you're a potential danger to your own safety or the safety of others. If they suspect you present a threat to a specific third person, they must alert that person.

- If you're using your insurance to pay for therapy, your therapist will probably have to provide them with information about your treatment, which will include a diagnosis. Mental health professionals use a diagnostic manual called the *Diagnostic and Statistical Manual* (DSM). You should know what diagnosis the insurance company is being given. In some cases, therapists have a choice of diagnoses, and you want to be sure they use the one that's the least severe while still being accurate. If you decide to use insurance, you are implicitly giving your therapist permission to furnish the necessary information.

- Therapists treating minor children have the right to share information with the children's parents (although they might not find it advisable to do so; see Chapter Eleven).

- Though therapy is considered legally "privileged," there are conditions under which therapists or their clinical records can be subpoenaed. If you're involved in a divorce or other legal proceeding and are concerned about confidentiality, check your local laws by calling your state department of mental health.

- Therapists may discuss their work with colleagues or supervisors for the purpose of furthering their education or providing you with better treatment. This is a good thing for you, because it means the therapist is working to maximize her own thinking and improve her work. If therapists do seek consultation, however, they must conceal your identity.

Truth in Advertising

You have a right to know the credentials and training of any therapist you consult. In turn, therapists have a responsibility to maintain every license they say they have. If you want to double-check, call the credentialing board (see the Resources section for contact information). The board can also tell you if a therapist has ever been sued for malpractice. Note: therapists are ethically bound not to provide any therapy for which they have not been trained. When in doubt, ask.

Dual Roles

Therapists should never become involved in any other relationship with their clients. For example, they should never go into business with a client, or provide treatment to a social acquaintance, employee, or family member. The therapeutic relationship is an intensely emotional involvement, and as such it carries a special vulnerability. At times, patients invest their therapists with a kind of parental authority; at other times they may have sexual feelings toward them. These feelings are an inevitable and integral part of the work, and are what make it possible to explore and understand a patient's way of being in relationships (see the explanation of "transference" on pages 68–69). When therapists exploit their role it not only compromises the work you're paying them to do with you, but often does real emotional harm.

Sex

The rule on sexual intimacy between therapists and their patients: *never.* This means *never under any circumstance*—there is no gray area. Violations of this taboo represent the most frequent complaints filed against therapists. Many more incidents probably go unreported because, like any sexual violation, they bring a sense of shame and guilt to the victim. Being sexually attracted to your therapist isn't inevitable, but it's normal and happens frequently. And since they're people, it would be preposterous to think that in the course of a career any therapist could avoid *ever* having sexual feelings for a patient. But having feelings is very different from acting on them.

You should know that:

- It's unethical for a therapist to have sexual contact with any patient, *including a former patient.*
- Your therapist is your therapist—no matter where you happen to be. If you meet your therapist at a party, he's bound by the same ethical code as in the office.
- In general, touching is not a part of therapy. A handshake is okay. A pat on the back, even an occasional hug, particularly when initiated by a child or at the termination of a long therapy, might be okay. But beyond that, no. The exception is in body therapy, where touch is an explicit part of the method, and the therapist can describe its role and its limits. In body therapy, too, sexual contact is explicitly unethical.
- If you think your therapist is sexually aroused or acting seductively, first try talking about it. Even if the feeling is really coming from you, a good therapist will want to explore it. If she gets defensive or dismisses your feelings, or if your discomfort persists over time, consider switching therapists or getting an outside consultation (see Chapter Ten).
- If your sex therapist ever offers him- or herself as a partner in sexual "exercises" or as a "sex surrogate," run. Unfortunately, such therapists are not likely to have broken any civil laws. But if they're certified by the American Association of Sex Educators, Counselors, and Therapists (AASECT), you should contact that organization to lodge a complaint. And if they're licensed in any discipline, contact the licensing board (see information on page 120).

Reliability

Your therapist has an ethical responsibility to protect the integrity of your therapy. This means that:

- Your therapist should maintain regular appointments, including starting and ending on time.
- Your therapist shouldn't allow intrusions or interruptions during your sessions (such as telephone calls), except in emergencies.
- Your therapist should behave in a professionally consistent way, meaning he shouldn't radically switch his approach midstream. In other words, a warm, supportive therapist shouldn't suddenly and permanently clam up. Someone who has been working with you for two years three times per week shouldn't precipitously recommend cutting down to once per week. Any changes in your treatment should be thoroughly discussed with and agreed to by you before they're made.

Respect

No therapist should ever use your therapy to further her own agenda. This means that:

- Your therapist has the responsibility to listen, pay attention, and be emotionally present during your sessions. It's inevitable that she'll have bad days from time to time, or that her mind will occasionally wander. But ethical therapists try to keep their attention focused on you, and when it does stray, they try to understand *why*. When a good therapist is momentarily distracted from you, it's usually in reaction to something going on in your treatment. She'll be able to make use of her reaction to understand you better.
- Your therapist should never advocate any moral, religious, or political position. Proselytizing has no place in therapy.
- Your therapist should never pronounce judgments about any aspect of your life, including your sexual orientation.

Free Choice

In most cases, therapy is purely voluntary, so:
- Your therapist can never force you to accept any form of treatment (including medication) you don't want, and should never attempt to do so. The exception is when your life or safety (or someone else's) is at stake.
- Your therapist can never prevent you from consulting another therapist for a second opinion, and should never try.
- Your therapist can't hold you in therapy longer than you wish to stay, and should never try.

Discrimination

While therapists in private practice can legally choose which patients to take (and should exclude those populations they're not qualified to help), they're ethically bound not to discriminate on the basis of race, religion, ethnicity, or other factors.

Lawful Behavior

Therapists are bound by the law of the land, just like everyone else. Therefore:

- Your therapist should never encourage you to perform any illegal activities.
- Your therapist should never encourage the use of illegal drugs.
- Your therapist should never commit insurance fraud, or encourage you to. For example, he should never bill your insurance company more than their actual fee, or bill for more or different services than were actually provided. Even if this is done to increase your reimbursement, breaking the law as a part of therapy is a fundamental compromise to the integrity of your work together.

IN THE unlikely event that you're the victim of unethical conduct on the part of a therapist, you'll need to lodge a complaint with the state licensing board for the discipline in which this therapist practices. There is some variation in the titles of these boards. For example, your state might call its regulatory body the "Department of Health and Mental Health," or the "Department of Health and Mental Hygiene." At any rate, you should be able to find it easily, and then you'll be able to narrow your search down to the discipline you're looking for (psychology, medicine, social work, nursing, marriage and family therapy, or counseling). And if your therapist is a member of a professional organization (such as the National Association of Social Workers, or the American Family Therapy Association), contact them, too.

If your therapist is unlicensed, you don't have much recourse. The exception is if your therapist has broken a civil law, such as using or suggesting you use illegal drugs (in which case you should contact the police), or committing insurance fraud (in which case you contact the insurance company).

Etiquette

Now that we've covered the black-and-white ethical issues, what about the shades of gray? In therapy, there are principles governing therapist behavior which, though not necessarily made explicit in the professional guidelines, are also critical to good treatment. These rules of therapy "etiquette" derive from solid clinical thinking about what works. Even though there will be some variation according to a practitioner's theoretical orientation and personality, well-trained and conscientious therapists know the rules and apply them in a professionally consistent way. In other words, the good ones don't "wing it." They make exceptions, or depart from normal etiquette, only when they think that to do so will serve their patients' best interest.

Personal Information about the Therapist

As I said, you have a right to information about your therapist's professional qualifications. But most therapists won't answer direct questions about their personal lives, such as whether or not they are married, or what their religion is. This doesn't mean they're aloof or withholding, or that they just like being mysterious. Therapists generally don't disclose personal information because to do so would intrude on your therapy (see Chapter Five). Therapists, especially those who work from a psychodynamic standpoint, want to leave room for you to feel about them any way you need to—free from distracting facts about their lives. For the same reason, most therapists don't display photographs of their families in their offices.

> **Most therapists won't answer direct questions about their personal lives, such as whether or not they are married, or what their religion is. This doesn't mean they're aloof or withholding, or that they just like being mysterious. Therapists generally don't disclose personal information because to do so would intrude on your therapy.**

Your therapist won't be a "blank screen" to you. You'll have lots of opportunities to observe things about her, for example a wedding ring or a recently acquired piece of art. If your therapist practices in a home office, you may even see members of her family in passing. Over time, you'll figure things out about your therapist's character, such as her values or sense of humor. Occasionally, your therapist may even choose to disclose some aspect of her life or experience. The key is that any self-disclosure on the part of your therapist should be done thoughtfully, with your best interests in mind. For example, if you've recently lost someone important to you and your therapist has planned a vacation, she might decide to tell you where she's going so you won't be as anxious about the separation.

Another exception to the self-disclosure rule is when there are circumstances in your therapist's life that will directly affect your therapy. If he misses a few sessions because of the flu, there's no need for you to know why. But if he's diagnosed with cancer and will have to miss many sessions because of radiation and chemotherapy, he should tell you so you can prepare emotionally. Similarly, if your therapist becomes pregnant and is planning maternity leave, she should give you as much advance notice as possible. Having this type of preparation doesn't preclude exploring your feelings about your therapist's absence (or illness, or pregnancy). It brings the issues into the therapy so you can talk about them.

Socializing with Your Therapist

Because of the ethical injunction against dual roles, therapists and their patients shouldn't socialize. However, from time to time, you may run into your therapist in a social setting—say, in a movie line or at the grocery store. Meeting each other outside the office, especially if you live in a small town or travel in the same social or professional circles, isn't uncommon. How should you act? How can you expect your therapist to act? The best way to handle these encounters is by being natural, but brief. If you meet your therapist at a party, he'll probably smile quickly, say "hello," and move on. He probably won't engage you in conversation or introduce you to the person he's talking to. He probably also won't abruptly flee the scene, and you don't need to either. Therapy is a part of life, and the outside world sometimes intrudes. You can talk about your feelings about the encounter later, in a session.

Telephone Contact

Therapists have varying policies on using the telephone (or these days, e-mail) in their practices. Some limit its use to emergencies and scheduling, meaning that, unless you have an urgent need, they only want you to call them to set up or change an appointment. Other therapists are happy to talk to their patients between sessions, and some even encourage telephone "check-ins." A patient's needs are also a factor; people who are highly anxious or depressed, or who are in crisis, may need to call their therapists more often than those who are more stable. It's common for therapists to approve phone contact if there's a period of emergency, such as a suicide risk.

In general, I believe therapy goes best when it can be contained within sessions. Having lots of extra telephone contact with your therapist can get in the way of learning to manage on your own, or can siphon off feelings that really need to be talked about in person. If you find yourself wanting to call your therapist a lot, it's probably time to talk about increasing the frequency of your appointments, at least for a while. Most therapists will suggest this, if it's hard for you to manage the interval between sessions.

While therapists should return calls promptly, not all will do so after work hours or on the weekends. So, if you think you'll want quick access, ask about this during your initial consultation. Also, therapists are entitled to charge for time spent on the phone that's not for routine scheduling, and some do. You should ask about that, too (see Chapter Eight).

Fees

Not all therapists are comfortable talking about fees. But they should be, because money is as big an issue in therapy as it is everywhere else. You should know, at the outset of treatment, what your fee will be, how frequently you'll be billed, and when you'll be expected to pay. There's a lot of variation among practitioners. Some bill at each session, others weekly or monthly. Some accept only checks, others cash and credit cards. Some will bill your insurance directly, others won't. If your therapist is hazy about her policies or lazy about enforcing them, there can be problems. If, for example, she forgets to bill you for a while or neglects to collect on an outstanding bill, and you get behind in your payments, you might feel anxious or guilty. Those feelings would get in the way of your therapy.

This doesn't mean there's no room for flexibility. Many therapists will let you pay late if you run into difficulty, or pay your bill over time. Others will consider a temporary or permanent reduction in your fee if your financial circumstances worsen. The main point is that any departure from the stated policy, or any feelings you have about the policy, should be out in the open. Money only becomes a problem when it's silently attached to secrets and shame.

Small Talk

In therapy you should talk about whatever's on your mind. Allowing your mind to wander freely is the way to learn about yourself. We call this "free association" (see Chapter Five). Say you come to therapy wanting to talk about a book you just read. Maybe you think the book is unimportant, and you're reluctant at first to share your ideas about it. But as you do, you realize that a character in the book reminds you a lot of someone important in your life. Then you're off to the races, thinking about yourself in new ways. Talking about ordinary things in life, especially the ones that at first seem trivial, is the way to tap into our unconscious thoughts and feelings.

On the other hand, some kinds of small talk indicate that therapy has gotten off track. If, for example, you find yourself chattering away in session without getting anywhere or feeling much of anything, you may be avoiding talking about something else. It's your therapist's job to comment on the moments when you seem emotionally distant or disconnected.

But what about small talk between you and your therapist? Some is inevitable. After all, there's a relationship between you, and you should expect normal human interactions. But certain therapists are "chattier" than others. They might tell you details about their lives or personal experiences which they think will be useful to you. The key questions are:

- Is the content of the session mainly directed by you?
- Does the therapist keep small talk to a minimum and only chime in with outside details or comments when it's in your best interest?
- Do you feel your therapist is professional, thoughtful, and serious about helping you?

If you can answer "yes" to all of these questions, then you're on firm footing.

What to Call Each Other

Some therapists like to be called by their titles (Dr. or Mr. So-and-So, and the like), others would rather be on a first-name basis with their patients. Most clinicians make their preferences clear, but if they don't, you should ask. Most therapists ask new patients how they would like to be addressed. Others are more formal and will use a title unless requested otherwise. From time to time a therapist who wants to be called by a title uses first names when speaking with patients—for instance when working with a couple or family. But this can be awkward, since it implies a power differential between therapist and patient. If this happens to you and you don't like it, bring it up for discussion.

Vacations

Some therapists take regular vacations every year (for example, the proverbial month of August that used to be a given), but most have varying schedules. Unless something unexpected comes up and your therapist has to be away suddenly, you should expect to be given ample notice. Obviously, you won't be charged when your therapist is away. Most (but not all) won't charge you for sessions missed during your vacations if you give adequate notice. Some, especially those doing more frequent weekly sessions, such as in psychoanalysis, will charge for missed sessions because they have an understanding that the time has been reserved for you. Be sure to check your therapist's policy to avoid misunderstandings.

Cancellation Policies

These vary widely. Some therapists don't charge at all for missed or cancelled sessions, others require twenty-four hours' notice or more, or charge for all sessions no matter what. But most therapists are humane in their application of policy. For example, even though there might be such a therapist, I don't know one who'd feel right about charging you for a session you missed because someone close to you died.

Emergency Coverage

Most therapists, when they go away, arrange for a colleague to be available to their patients in case of emergency. Of course, this covering therapist won't know you, so will be of limited usefulness. In any case, if you're worried about emergencies when your therapist is away, ask what arrangements have been made. If there's no one covering the practice, you and your therapist can make another contingency plan.

Gifts

Is it OK to give your therapist a gift? Most would prefer you didn't. Still, there are no hard and fast rules. While it would be wildly inappropriate for you to buy your therapist a television or piece of jewelry, a keepsake such as a picture you painted or a photograph you took, which had special meaning for your work together, might be fine. The important thing about any gift you give your therapist, whether it is accepted or not, is that the two of you understand its symbolic value and why you want to give it.

Do therapists give gifts? No. The exception can be in child therapy. Many therapists, including me, like to give small gifts to their child patients at special times, like birthdays or the end of treatment. Because they're young, children expect and need evidence of their own importance to the people who are important to them, including their therapists.

Referring Friends and Family Members to Your Therapist

There's a huge gray area around therapists' taking on new patients with connections to existing ones. In general, I don't think it's a good idea to take on a family member or friend of a current client, because it compromises that client's privacy and creates competitive feelings. Of course, there are exceptions. Sometimes an individual therapy will expand to couple or family therapy. At other times, it's financially or logistically expedient for the same therapist to work with more than one sibling in a family, either together or individually.

There are other exceptions. Sometimes therapists take on new patients without knowing in advance that there's a connection to an existing patient. And in small towns there aren't always enough therapists to go around. In some settings, such as school counseling centers, inpatient treatment centers, and some clinics, therapists are shared by many patients who tend to know each other. And some group therapists also see their group members in individual therapy, so it's clear that the group members do know each other.

Whatever the situation, you should feel that your therapist respects you and your confidentiality. Talk to your therapist about any feelings you have about another of her patients—even if it's only someone you glimpsed briefly in the waiting room—in the same way that you talk about anything else.

The Couch or the Chair?

Most (though not all) people in analysis lie on a couch, because it helps them to relax, frees them from the distractions of the analyst's facial expressions, and encourages free association. But lying down can also engender feelings of physical and emotional vulnerability. Psychoanalysis can handle these feelings, because of its frequency and the intensity of the relationship between patient and analyst. But ordinary therapy can't, so it should be done sitting up. If you're not in three to five times-per-week psychoanalysis and your therapist recommends you lie down on a couch, inquire about his training and whether it included the use of the couch. If you have doubts, get a consultation. For a fuller discussion of this issue see Chapter Ten.

Obviously, I haven't covered—and couldn't possibly cover—every aspect of therapy that might seem new, strange, or confusing. By now I've said this enough that I hope you're getting the idea: if you have a question or concern about an aspect of your therapy or your therapist's behavior, *bring it up directly.* You'll usually learn something not only about your therapist, but about yourself. If you don't get satisfaction from the discussion, get an outside consultation.

PATIENT'S BILL OF RIGHTS

IN 1997, a group of nine allied mental health organizations came together to develop a shared set of principles regarding Americans' rights to quality mental health care. At a press conference on February 20th, they delivered the following document:

Principles for the Provision of Mental Health and Substance Abuse Treatment Services

A Bill of Rights

Our commitment is to provide quality mental health and substance abuse services to all individuals without regard to race, color, religion, national origin, gender, age, sexual orientation, or disabilities.

1. Right to Know

- **Benefits:** Individuals have the right to be provided information from the purchasing entity (such as employer or union or public purchaser) and the insurance/third party payer describing the nature and extent of their mental health and substance abuse treatment benefits. This information should include details on procedures to obtain access to services, on utilization management procedures, and on appeal rights. The information should be presented clearly in writing with language that the individual can understand.

- **Professional Expertise:** Individuals have the right to receive full information from the potential treating professional about that professional's knowledge, skills, preparation, experience, and credentials. Individuals have the right to be informed about the options available for treatment interventions and the effectiveness of the recommended treatment.

- **Contractual Limitations:** Individuals have the right to be informed by the treating professional of any arrangements, restrictions, and/or covenants established between the third party payer and the treating professional that could interfere with or influence treatment recommendations. Individuals have the right to be informed of the nature of information that may be disclosed for the purposes of paying benefits.
- **Appeals and Grievances:**
    1. Individuals have the right to be provided information about the procedures they can use to appeal benefit utilization decisions to the third party payer systems, to the employer or purchasing entity, and to external regulatory entities.
    2. Individuals have the right to receive information about the methods they can use to submit complaints or grievances regarding provision of care by the treating professional to that profession's regulatory board and to the professional association.

2. Confidentiality

Individuals have the right to be guaranteed the protection of the confidentiality of their relationship with their mental health and substance abuse professional, except when laws or ethics dictate otherwise. Any disclosure to another party will be time limited and made with the full written, informed consent of the individuals. Individuals shall not be required to disclose confidential, privileged or other information other than: diagnosis, prognosis, type of treatment, time and length of treatment, and cost.

- Entities receiving information for the purpose of benefits determination, public agencies receiving information for health care planning, or any other organization with legitimate right to information will maintain clinical information in confidence with the same rigor and be subject to the same penalties for violation as is the direct provider of care.
- Information technology will be used for transmission, storage, or data management only with methodologies that remove individual identifying information and assure the protection of the

individual's privacy. Information should not be transferred, sold or otherwise utilized.

3. Choice

Individuals have the right to choose any duly licensed/certified professional for mental health and substance abuse services. Individuals have the right to receive full information regarding the education and training of professionals, treatment options (including risks and benefits), and cost implications to make an informed choice regarding the selection of care deemed appropriate by individual and professional.

4. Determination of Treatment

Recommendations regarding mental health and substance abuse treatment shall be made only by a duly licensed/certified professional in conjunction with the individual and his or her family as appropriate. Treatment decisions should not be made by third party payers. The individual has the right to make final decisions regarding treatment.

5. Parity

Individuals have the right to receive benefits for mental health and substance abuse treatment on the same basis as they do for any other illnesses, with the same provisions, co-payments, lifetime benefits, and catastrophic coverage in both insurance and self-funded/self-insured health plans.

6. Discrimination

Individuals who use mental health and substance abuse benefits shall not be penalized when seeking other health insurance or disability, life or any other benefit.

7. Benefit Usage

The individual is entitled to the entire scope of the benefits within the benefit plan that will address his or her clinical needs.

8. Benefit Design

Whenever both federal and state law and/or regulations are applicable, the professional and all payers shall use whichever affords the individual the greatest level of protection and access.

9. Treatment Review

To assure that treatment review processes are fair and valid, individuals have the right to be guaranteed that any review of their mental health and substance abuse treatment shall involve a professional having the training, credentials and licensure required to provide the treatment in the jurisdiction in which it will be provided. The reviewer should have no financial interest in the decision and is subject to the section on confidentiality.

10. Accountability

Treating professionals may be held accountable and liable to individuals for any injury caused by gross incompetence or negligence on the part of the professional. The treating professional has the obligation to advocate for and document necessity of care and to advise the individual of options if payment authorization is denied. Payers and other third parties may be held accountable and liable to individuals for any injury caused by gross incompetence or negligence or by their clinically unjustified decisions.

Sponsoring Organizations:

- American Association for Marriage and Family Therapy
- American Counseling Association
- American Family Therapy Academy
- American Nurses Association
- American Psychological Association
- American Psychiatric Association
- American Psychiatric Nurses Association
- National Association of Social Workers
- National Federation of Societies for Clinical Social Work

In addition to the nine signatories on the Mental Health Bill of Rights, several other important groups added their support:

- National Mental Health Association
- American Group Psychotherapy Association
- American Psychoanalytic Association
- National Association of Alcoholism and Drug Abuse Counselors
- National Depressive and Manic Depressive Association

TEN

Is This Working?

ONCE YOU'VE STARTED with a therapist, what can you expect? Will you be able to tell if you've chosen a gem, or is there a chance you'll get stuck with a lemon? Will you know instinctively whether or not you're making progress, or will you fall under a hypnotic spell? Will you know when you're done, or will you live forever in the land of eternal therapy?

Your relationship with your therapist has a life span. Whether this is six weeks or six years, it will go through a series of developmental stages. Like you, your therapy doesn't develop in a straight line—feelings and symptoms come and go, and progress has to be measured over time. Still, there are some recognizable guideposts you can use to gauge how well things are going.

Therapists talk about three "stages" of treatment: the "beginning," "middle," and "termination" (or ending) phase. Let's look at the typical characteristics of each phase, so you'll be familiar with them.

The Beginning Phase

At the start of therapy, you'll probably feel relief. You'll finally have someone to talk to, and you'll be hopeful of getting help. If you've been suffering from troubling symptoms, such as anxiety or depression, you may find they lessen considerably. Difficult circumstances and events may not cause you to feel as stressed as they used to. Problems in relationships outside of therapy aren't resolved right away, of course, but you may find that some of them calm down. For example, if you're in marital therapy, the two of you may stop fighting so often or so intensely. This may be because you're feeling closer (you're doing something important together, after all), or because you keep disagreements from escalating until they can be discussed in sessions.

During this phase you may feel very positive toward your therapist. You've chosen someone you like, and there's a sense of newness and adventure. Your therapist will seem (and, hopefully, will *be*) smart and supportive. He or she will help you see yourself in new ways. Together you'll make new connections between your past and your present, and develop new insights. This isn't to say that even in the beginning you won't ever feel irritated, angry, or critical of your therapist, especially if those are ways you often feel about people. But many clinicians describe the beginning of treatment as a "honeymoon phase." You and your therapist are still getting to know each other, and are still free of a history that might include painful feelings and experiences. It's normal, and even necessary, to idealize your therapist a bit in the beginning. This lets the relationship get going. It's a bit like getting married—no one would be able to take the leap if they couldn't temporarily suppress their negative feelings about their partner and focus on the good ones.

The Middle Phase

At some point the honeymoon will usually end. You may feel you've "hit a wall"; you've just stopped getting better. You may even begin to feel worse. You may ask yourself, "What am I doing wrong? Have I gone as far as I can? Did I choose a bad therapist? Are we incompatible?" These feelings are probably a good sign that you've come face to face with something important. It means your troubles have worked their way into your therapy, where they belong.

> **At some point the honeymoon will usually end. You may feel you've "hit a wall"; you've just stopped getting better. You may even begin to feel worse. You may ask yourself, "What am I doing wrong? Have I gone as far as I can? Did I choose a bad therapist? Are we incompatible?" These feelings are probably a good sign that you've come face to face with something important. It means your troubles have worked their way into your therapy, where they belong.**

All of us are made up of layers of feelings and experiences. The more painful a feeling or memory is, the deeper it's buried. The beginning phase of therapy deals mainly with the top layers. The memories and feelings contained in these layers, though often painful, are relatively easy to access and to tolerate. Remember: change is hard. As more painful feelings and memories come to the surface, our unconscious minds go into evasive maneuvers to protect our conscious minds. Therapists call these maneuvers "resistances"—the ways we reflexively feel and act in the effort to keep painful thoughts safely buried away. Unfortunately, resistances hurt more then they help, since whatever is kept out of our conscious minds is not available to be worked on and changed. Part of your work in therapy will be to face your resistances and work through them, so you can reach the parts of you that lie beneath.

Some common forms of resistance are negative feelings about therapy and the therapist. This means that as you move into the middle phase of treatment, where you'll have to deal with more problematic areas of your personality, you may find yourself suddenly questioning various aspects of your treatment. Basically you should still trust your therapist. But while you used to think she was brilliant, now she might sometimes seem dull and slow on the uptake, or somehow critical of you. While you used to look forward to sessions, now they might sometimes seem like a pointless chore.

This type of resistance is inevitable, but it's only helpful if you can talk about it. Tell your therapist about any negative feelings you're having so you can explore them together. If, for example, you think she's cold and unresponsive, if you're mad because you think she has unfairly charged you for a missed session, or if you simply think she's not doing anything for you—tell her. Even if she doesn't come right out and agree with you, a good therapist should be receptive, empathic, and interested in exploring your feelings.

On the other hand, not all your negative feelings toward your therapist will be resistances. If your therapist has made a mistake or contributed to a problem in his relationship with you, he should admit it. And the good ones will. But what if you bring up your feelings of irritation, anger, or frustration, and he acts dismissive or insists the problem is all in you? Or what if you have what feels like a productive conversation, but over time you continue to feel disgruntled? How can you tell for sure if the feeling is coming from you or from a behavior in your therapist? How can you decide whether or not the two of you are compatible? Here are some guidelines for deciding whether negative feelings derive from your own resistance or from problems in the therapy itself.

Signs of Resistance

- Everything in your therapy is going along fine, then *boom*—suddenly you feel angry or bored.
- You have nothing to talk about (although silence is a normal part of therapy).
- You find yourself feeling suddenly and completely better.
- You find yourself forgetting appointments, or finding reasons to cancel them.
- Other things in your life suddenly seem to be more important than therapy.

- You start to keep secrets from your therapist.
- You begin to feel you can't afford therapy, even though your finances haven't changed substantially.

Signs That the Problem May Be with the Therapist

- Your therapist becomes angry when you voice doubts about her.
- Your therapist quickly attributes your feelings to resistance without exploring them.
- Your therapist is critical of you for having negative feelings.
- Your therapist insists the problem is *you* when it clearly isn't (for example, he falls asleep in session, but denies it and says, "You *believe* I'm falling asleep because you think you're boring and unworthy of my attention.").
- Your therapist forgets appointments, is often late, takes telephone calls during sessions with you, or reschedules frequently.
- You have a sense that your therapist isn't too emotionally well-glued (for example, he has poor hygiene, dresses or behaves bizarrely or inappropriately, or has strange habits or tics).
- You consistently feel that your therapist doesn't "get you," and no amount of talking about the problem seems to help.
- You feel stuck—you're just not moving forward anymore.
- You always feel worse after sessions, especially about *yourself* (this is different from simply feeling sad or stirred up after discussing painful topics).
- Your therapist is pressuring you into talking about things you don't want to talk about, or into staying in therapy when you want to leave.

Getting a Consultation

If you've reached a stalemate or are questioning whether or not to continue with your therapist, it may be time to get an independent consultation. This type of consultation is different from the kind in which you interview potential therapists. This is more like a second opinion. You bring your problem to another, preferably quite experienced, clinician for clarification and advice on how and whether to continue with your current practitioner. If you think you need a consultation, bring it up with your therapist. He should be open to exploring the possibility, and even willing to suggest a senior colleague. Ideally, he'll be supportive (and maybe even participate), but even if he's not, he shouldn't try to stop you or get in your way.

THE THERAPY CONSULTATION

YOU'VE REACHED an impasse with your therapist, and you're wondering whether to continue with her. How do you go about finding a professional to consult with, and how should you conduct yourself during the consultation?

■ Find a senior therapist.

You want someone with a lot of experience. Use the steps for finding a therapist that I outlined in Chapter Seven, but make sure you ask each potential therapist how long he or she has been in practice. Pick one who's been at it ten years or longer.

■ Tell the new therapist that you want a consultation, not therapy.

In your initial telephone call, explain to the new person that you're not necessarily looking to switch therapists but want an independent consultation to sort through the issues. Most therapists will be fine with that, but you should check up-front. You can always decide later if you want to switch to a new therapist (maybe to the consultant).

■ Beware of consultants who are too quick to judgment.

Most problems that arise between therapists and their clients are not black and white. For example, say you're seeking a consultation because you think your therapist is cold and unresponsive. You may be right. On the other hand, it could be that you have a tendency to view all the people you're close to in this way. And the two are not mutually exclusive. Perhaps your therapist's naturally cool demeanor is a bad fit for you, or perhaps your demands for more input are pushing your therapist into a more reserved position. A good consultant will take the time to understand the complexities of your situation, including both your and your therapist's contributions. On the other hand, if your therapist is behaving in an ethically inappropriate way, a good consultant will tell you that right away.

■ **Beware of consultants who try to woo you away.**

Assuming you've been clear up-front about what you want, a consultation should be just that. The consultant should respect your existing relationship with your therapist. Any decision to switch should be yours, and not coerced.

Ending therapy

Unless your therapy was always meant to be short-term, the decision to end should come about gradually. You'll have experienced a lot of changes. Perhaps you'll have noticed yourself letting go of old grudges or not dwelling so intensely on past injuries. A frequent sign of being ready to stop therapy is feeling better about your parents, even if they were less than ideal. Maybe you'll find yourself taking more pleasure in your life and your relationships, or maybe the symptoms that brought you to therapy have been resolved. You'll have learned and integrated new ways of feeling and thinking, so when you hit a bumpy patch in the road you can navigate it without falling apart. You'll be feeling ready to try life on your own.

> **A frequent sign of being ready to stop therapy is feeling better about your parents, even if they were less than ideal.**

You'll also notice shifts in your attitudes toward your therapist. Over time, the knowledge that he's just a regular person—with positive and negative attributes—will really *sink in*. Your feelings toward him won't feel as intense as they once did. His approval won't seem as crucial, so when the two of you disagree it'll be easier for you to speak up. When he disappoints you or lets you down, you won't feel as angry or upset. Your therapist, and your relationship with him, will seem more like a part of real life. I used to joke that I knew that I was ready to end my analysis when my analyst stopped looking like Clint Eastwood and started looking like Don Knotts.

It's best when you and your therapist can agree on a time to end, but it doesn't always happen that way. Regardless, you should take plenty of time to discuss the issue and to understand your reasons for ending. Once you've decided to stop, you and your therapist will set a date sometime in the future. You'll need time, ideally several weeks or months (depending on how long you've been in therapy), to prepare. You'll want to review your progress and consolidate your gains. You'll want to talk about the future, so you can anticipate challenges that might come up and strategize ways of managing them.

Even if you feel confident about your decision, you'll probably get cold feet at some point. You may find that old feelings, problems, or symptoms come back, or that new ones crop up at the eleventh hour. None of these things necessarily indicates that you're making a mistake. The end of therapy inevitably evokes feelings left over from other endings and leave-takings you've been through—both good and bad. If you were a child of divorce, part of you will feel like one again. If you've lost a spouse, you'll grieve anew. The termination phase offers a chance to review the gains of therapy because the fact of ending introduces its own anxieties, and these echo with the ones that brought you in the first place. That's why this phase is so useful, and why you need plenty of time for it. The ending of therapy is the ending of a close relationship, so it's often painful. But since it's a *planned* ending, it's available for you to look at and understand, and it offers an opportunity for you to work through issues of loss and separation in a new and renewing way.

> **Even if you feel confident about your decision, you'll probably get cold feet at some point. You may find that old feelings, problems, or symptoms come back, or that new ones crop up at the eleventh hour. None of these things necessarily indicates that you're making a mistake.**

Staying in Touch

After you stop, you may want to be in touch with your former therapist from time to time. If something important happens, like a marriage, a baby, or a new job, you might want to write to her. Your therapist will be emotionally invested in you, and even though she won't initiate contact, she'll appreciate hearing how you're getting along.

ELEVEN

Child Therapy

WE ALL WANT desperately to do a good job as parents. We want our kids to be happy, well adjusted, and successful. Since our children don't come with user's manuals, the best we can do is try to replicate the good qualities of our own childhoods and correct the bad ones. If we experienced our own parents as available and nurturing, we want to offer those same qualities to our own children. If we didn't, we want to do better. But despite our best efforts, our kids occasionally run into problems. Sometimes these problems are due to circumstances beyond our control, such as the death of a parent or a childhood illness. At other times the reasons aren't so clear; we see our children struggling and we don't know why. In either case we're likely to feel frightened and guilty. We might ask, "Is it my fault? Where did I go wrong?" Because we want so much for our children and love them so much, it can sometimes be hard to sort our own worries out from the real difficulties our children are experiencing, and to figure out how and when to intercede.

Each developmental stage of childhood has its own tasks. The work of the child at each phase is to master new skills and to integrate them into a growing sense of self. Healthy kids get excited about learning and becoming more independent, but the changes they experience are bittersweet. Along with the part of them that longs for the next thing—whether it is learning how to walk or talk, go on a first sleepover, or drive a car—there's a normal part of them that clings wistfully to the past, to a time when they were more dependent on you.

So a certain amount of struggle is inevitable in childhood. If you've ever had a child in the "terrible twos," you're familiar with the tantrum that can ensue when a toddler wants to "do it myself," but isn't quite up to the task. If you've ever sent a child off to preschool, you may have witnessed your three-year-old trading his excitement and confidence for clinging and sobbing as you attempted to say good-bye at the door. The vacillation between sullen rejection and cuddliness that teenagers often display toward their parents is another indication of ambivalence while growing up.

One of our key jobs as parents is to facilitate our kids' successful negotiation of each developmental stage. We do this by helping them bear the anxiety of leaving their baby parts behind, and by support-ing the part of them striving to be more grown-up. This means that we often have to resist the urge to rush in too quickly to help. Some-times we have to emotionally sit on our hands and allow our children to struggle a bit on their own. In popular psychology this has some-times been called "tough love"—the ability to support our children's growth by giving them the emotional space they need to grapple with and master the work of growing up.

So how do you know when your child is displaying the normal ups and downs of childhood, and when it's time to intervene and seek outside help? To figure this out, you must first have an idea of what you can normally expect your child to be working on and what behaviors you might expect to see at each developmental stage. Much of this information will be familiar to you, but let's review.

Your Child's Development

The First Year

The baby's developmental task in the first year is to form a safe and secure attachment to its primary care-taker (for simplicity's sake, let's call it the mother). This good attachment is based on the mother's being attuned to the needs of her child and responding to them empathically. The baby cries, so his mother cuddles him, guesses that he's hungry and offers the breast or bottle. When he screws up his nose and turns away, she realizes that he is not hungry, but sleepy. Cooing, she places him in his crib. Thus, the mother takes in her baby's communications, makes sense of them, and responds to them as successfully as she can. Over time and thousands of such interactions, the baby develops a feeling that the world is a safe and predictable place. This feeling of basic trust serves as the bedrock for the growing baby's subsequent developmental tasks. Struggles around eating and sleeping are common in the first year, as you adjust to your baby's temperament and work out daily rhythms.

The Toddler

Now your baby can walk and talk, which means she can begin to assert her own will in new ways. "Do it myself" and "No, no, no" are common refrains as your child struggles to define herself, and temper tantrums are common as she confronts her own physical and emotional limitations. During this phase your child must learn to modulate her own aggressive and assertive impulses. That is, she has to learn to cope with the angry feelings she sometimes has, and to deal with limits (her own, as well as those imposed by you). Some struggles around toilet training, learning to dress, and sharing with others are normal at this age.

Another important task is to be able to tolerate longer separations from you. Just as your small child has a life away from Mommy and Daddy, so do you have a life apart from her. As she uses her new mobility to move away from you and back, in increasingly larger circles, she must be able to hold onto the idea of you in her mind as someone who loves her even when you're out of sight or when you fail to meet her requests (which you inevitably sometimes will and should). It's normal at this age for your child to display worry at times of separation.

The Preschool Child

Now your child must adjust to the move beyond the sphere of your family, into day care, nursery school, and (eventually) kindergarten. Huge developments in his cognitive capacities mean that he can now "symbolize." His dawning ability to form and hold abstract concepts in mind allows for the emergence of pre-reading (he'll be reading by first or second grade) and rich imaginative play. It also means that your child will likely experience new or heightened anxieties. Fear of the dark, of monsters hiding under the bed, spiders, and the like are not uncommon. As your child's life away from home becomes more complex and demanding, he might exhibit some heightened separation anxiety, particularly around going to school. Especially if a new child joins the family, your three- to six-year-old might briefly return to behaviors he had grown out of, such as angry outbursts, difficulty in being away from you, bedwetting, or difficulty sleeping.

The School-Age Child

As your child moves into elementary school, she works to solidify her accomplishments from earlier periods: basic trust, separation, and managing anger and her destructive impulses (we all have them!). A major task of this phase is the consolidation of gender identity (a boy knowing he is a boy, a girl knowing she is a girl), and developing a beginning sense of right and wrong. Peer relationships move front and center, and your child must balance her preoccupation with friends with the growing academic demands of school. Problems at this age tend to cluster around your child's adjustment to the larger social world. Any learning difficulties will probably make themselves known at this point, although more subtle ones may show up as late as high school, and in some cases even in college.

Adolescence

Like the toddler, the adolescent must grapple with issues of separation and autonomy. Ambivalence toward his parents' values and a retreat into intimate peer relationships help him manage his anxiety about leaving home for the larger world. Social experimentation (and some acting out) also facilitates the tasks of this period, which include consolidation of sexual identity and orientation, the capacity for moral and ethical judgment, and the beginnings of an individual set of life values.

When to Get Professional Help

In childhood—in fact, throughout life—development is not linear. You can expect to see your child struggle as he or she learns to master new challenges. Some backsliding in development is normal, even necessary, as your child grows older. So how can you decide whether your child's difficulties fall within the normal range or not? Here are some clues that it's time to see a therapist for a consultation:

- Your child's symptoms aren't transient, but persist over months.
- Your child's symptoms interfere with his or her normal functioning (at home, at school, or with peers).
- Your child's symptoms interfere with the normal functioning of your family.
- You feel angry, exhausted, and disappointed in your child a lot of the time.
- You find you don't like your child, even though you may be too ashamed to admit it.
- You've felt for a long time that something is wrong.
- Trusted others have expressed concern.
- Your child has ever been physically or sexually abused.

Now let's look at some of the specific problems that should prompt you to consider therapy for your child:

- Problems with eating or sleeping (including nightmares that don't go away)
- Excessive difficulty with separations
- A consistently sad or melancholy mood
- Physical complaints with no distinguishable cause (such as stomach aches or headaches) that don't go away with easy reassurance
- Disinterest in friends, or trouble getting along with peers
- Bullying
- Being bullied or often being a victim
- Deteriorating school performance
- Difficulty concentrating
- Agitation or fidgetiness
- Extreme or unrealistic anxieties, fears, or phobias
- Excessive or public masturbation (childhood masturbation is normal, but should be in private)
- Accident proneness
- Low self-esteem
- Fatigue or apathy
- Aggressive behaviors toward self or others (such as biting, hitting, or scratching)
- Cruel behaviors (such as torturing animals)
- Risky, or acting-out behaviors (such as lighting fires)
- Constant rudeness and "talking back"
- Defiance of authority (such as disregard for school rules, skipping school, or ignoring curfews)
- Heavy drinking
- Drug use
- Excessive lying
- Stealing
- Obsessive or compulsive rituals (such as hand washing or pulling out hair)
- Preoccupation with death
- Wishing to die

Childhood Depression and Suicidality

Childhood depression is a very real problem. One of the difficulties in recognizing it is that children rarely express their feelings directly. Sometimes a child will report that he is sad, will cry a lot, or will simply *appear* chronically sad (for example, by wearing a sad expression, failing to make eye contact, or having a depressed-seeming body posture). Most of the time, though, children express their feelings indirectly. If your child tends to get hurt frequently, acts recklessly, has difficulty concentrating, is often irritable, or exhibits changes of eating and sleeping habits, you should consider getting help. But if your child ever expresses the wish to die or the feeling that life is not worth living, *get help right away.*

Some Special Considerations

Problems in Infancy

If you've ever had a baby, you know they are born very much *people,* that is, they bring to the world their own characteristics. Some are comfortable spending long periods of time lying in their cribs, happily watching the play of light on the ceiling; others seem always to want to be held. Some babies feed easily and stop when they are full; others fuss at the bottle or breast and resist being placed on a feeding schedule. Sometimes there's a good and natural "fit" between a baby's characteristics and those of its parent. For example, a colicky baby who cries at night might be luckily matched with a night-owl mother who's not rattled by late crying jags. Other times the fit isn't so good. For example, a baby who needs frequent holding and rocking might be matched with a mother who's not comfortable with a lot of physical contact.

Even when the natural fit between mother and baby isn't good, things can go fine. The mother in the above example could override her discomfort in favor of the baby's need for lots of holding and rocking, because she knows it's good for him. And the baby, too, could learn to tolerate more time on its own. Mostly, mothers and babies work things out in their relationship. Sometimes, though, it's more difficult for them to establish a rapport. When mothers feel unable to comfort their babies (and therefore unable to get relief from their demands), they can become locked in a cycle of frustration and guilt.

There are mother/infant specialists who can help you sort out difficulties you might be experiencing with your infant. Sometimes the root of the problem is physical. This need not be serious; perhaps your baby is milk- or wheat-intolerant, and a referral to a pediatric gastroenterologist is all you need. At other times, what's required is a better understanding of the issues around the fit between you and your baby, so you can recognize the feelings your baby's behavior stirs up in you. All parents of infants are often exhausted and, at times, anxious. But if you have persistent concerns, consult a specialist. If the specialist says there's nothing to worry about, you'll feel better. Here are some examples of problems that suggest a consultation is a good idea:

- You having trouble establishing a feeding or sleeping schedule for your baby.
- You feel more worn out by your baby's demands than you suspect is normal.
- You worry that your baby is stiff or unresponsive to you.
- It's hard for you to enjoy being with your baby.
- You're uninterested in playing with your baby, or unable to do so.
- You and your partner argue a lot about how to care for your baby.
- You're having a hard time getting your baby to eat or nurse in a sufficiently nourishing way.

When You Suspect Your Child Has Attention-Deficit Hyperactivity Disorder (ADHD)

Normal children, especially young ones, are often easily distracted, impulsive, and rambunctious. Adults have varying abilities to tolerate disruptive or highly active children; what's considered spirited fun by one parent might be considered chaos by another. Also, parents and teachers may disagree. If a teacher or school psychologist tells you your child has ADHD, don't take it as gospel. But if you've been wondering if your child is feeling or acting out of control, or you've been hearing such reports from other sources (friends, team coaches), it would be wise to get a consultation.

Here are some signs to look for:

- Your child always seems to be getting in trouble.
- He can't sit still.
- He is constantly moving from one game or toy to another.
- He interrupts constantly.
- He often does things he's been told not to do.
- He behaves in risky or impulsive ways, beyond the norm of the other kids.
- He has a hard time making friends.
- He's disorganized and constantly losing things.
- He often tells you he's stupid or bad.
- He has trouble calming down when he's upset.

Where to Go for Help

If you suspect your child has ADHD, your first stop should be the office of a psychologist who can do diagnostic testing to tease out the biological and emotional roots of your child's problem. Take some time in making your choice; not all psychologists are equally sophisticated. Many psychologists do lots of testing, and for some of them it becomes rote. You want one who is going to take the time to get to know your child well and provide you with a comprehensive and descriptive report of the test findings, not simply a rehashed version of a standard report with lots of technical jargon. Psychological testing is expensive, often hundreds or even thousands of dollars. So when your child's school psychologist can do it for free, it can be tempting to go that route. Some school psychologists are gifted and dedicated. But if you can afford a more expensive alternative, don't automatically choose the cheapest one. Your child's treatment plan will be based on the psychologist's report, so this is not a good place to pinch pennies.

Symptoms of ADHD can just as easily be caused by psychological factors as by biological ones. A child who is easily distracted or disruptive in school could, for example, be anxious about his parents' rocky marriage or a recent move that disrupted the family. Also, biological and emotional contributions are not mutually exclusive. Not only can they coexist, but a biological problem can sometimes lead to an emotional one. Children who have difficulty behaving appropriately often suffer from low self-esteem, anxiety, or depression as a consequence.

Medication on its own is rarely adequate in the treatment of ADHD. Even if your testing psychologist recommends a medication consultation with a child psychiatrist, consider starting with a talk therapist, either instead or in addition. Or, find a psychiatrist who could medicate if necessary but who will start with therapy. Medication can be useful in cases where therapy alone doesn't do the trick, but it should rarely be the first thing you try.

When You Suspect Developmental Delays or Learning Disabilities

Perhaps you're worried that your child is behind or struggling to keep up in some developmental area. Maybe your preschooler has trouble holding a crayon, or your first-grader is awkward in gym. Or maybe you suspect learning problems; your second-grader still isn't reading, or your fourth-grader can't master basic math. Unevenness is the rule in child development, and yours is probably better than other children at some things and not as good in others. If you have worries about any area of your child's development or learning, you should first speak with the teacher. If the teacher corroborates your concerns, you'll know to get testing. But even good teachers sometimes miss more subtle problems, or minimize them in an attempt to spare you worry. This is especially true, for instance, when a child is so bright that she exceeds minimal expectations even though she's struggling, or when the teacher is distracted by more troubled or disruptive kids. If your child's teacher reassures you that everything's fine or that your child will outgrow the problems, but you're still worried—get testing. It's worth the peace of mind.

Finally, if your child keeps telling you that he's stupid or can't do things the other kids can, pay attention and get him tested. All kids have bad days, but if you get the feeling your child really feels bad about himself, don't wait. If there's a developmental or learning problem, you'll find it. And if there isn't, you'll know your child's worries need addressing from an emotional angle, perhaps in therapy. Either way, your child will appreciate your taking his feelings seriously.

The Top Ten Misguided Reasons for Avoiding Child Therapy

Most caring, careful parents don't think twice about whisking their child off to the pediatrician if they suspect an ear infection. But when it comes to consulting a professional about their children's emotional health, many of these same parents remain reluctant. In working with many families over the years, I've found that what holds many parents back from getting help is fear and misinformation. Here are some of the most common reasons that parents give for not getting a therapy consultation for their child, and why we need to take another look at them.

1. Therapists always blame the parents.

It's hard to admit that something is bothering your child that you can't fix. For some people, asking for help feels like admitting failure. You should know that therapists aren't interested in blame, they're interested in understanding. Parenting is a complicated business, and when something goes wrong there are always several contributing factors. The idea in child therapy isn't to point the finger at you, the parent, and say you've screwed up. A good therapist knows you know your child best and you're doing the best you can. After all, you live with your child, while a therapist sees him for only a few hours a month. Depending on your child's age, you'll be more or less directly involved in the treatment. But just as in adult therapy, you and your child's therapist must be allies and collaborators if the work is to succeed.

> **The idea in child therapy isn't to point the finger at you, the parent, and say you've screwed up.**

On the other hand, we all know that parents sometimes do contribute to their children's problems. We're all familiar with the notion that people who were abused as children often grow up to be abusive parents. Sometimes the effects of our own early experience are this direct; we are influenced so strongly by our parents' behaviors that we repeat them unintentionally—even when we are determined not to. At other times, our parents' influence is more subtle. I mentioned at the start of this chapter that we all try to build on our own parents' strengths and correct their weaknesses. But no matter how much we try to be like or different from our own parents, they assert powerful unconscious influences on us. The result can be that we parent in ways that are unconscious reactions to our own parents.

Consider the Bloom family. Mr. and Mrs. Bloom brought their eight-year-old son, Aaron, to see me because he was afraid to sleep alone and could not get off to school on time. They described how he delayed bedtime by insisting that his mother help him with his unfinished homework. When she finally got him to bed at ten or eleven o'clock, he would not allow her to leave his room until he fell asleep. By that time, Mr. Bloom was fuming. He felt that his wife overindulged their son, and that she was neglecting their marriage by spending so much time with Aaron at night. Mr. Bloom did not intervene, however, and when he was critical, Mrs. Bloom would angrily retort, "I don't see you doing anything to help."

Mornings were not much better. Aaron, who was chronically sleep-deprived, had trouble waking up. His parents' gentle prodding soon gave way to whining, then desperate bribes, and, eventually, flat-out yelling. When they finally dragged him out of bed, he refused to dress himself. By the time Aaron ate breakfast, he had missed the school bus. His parents, now late for work, would drive him to school.

In sessions with Mr. and Mrs. Bloom, I learned that Mrs. Bloom's mother had been cold and aloof, and that she had also had a

schizophrenic brother whose frequent psychotic breaks had traumatized the family. Mr. Bloom, on the other hand, reported that his
childhood was "perfect." But when I pressed him a bit, he admitted
that his father had been a passive man, and that his mother had been
embarrassed by her husband's lack of ambition or contribution to
parenting their children.

As we talked, it became clear that Mrs. Bloom, who had felt
deprived of her mother's love as a child, wanted her own child always
to feel loved and nurtured. When her son cried out for her at night,
she was filled with sympathy ("I know what it feels like to be alone")
and guilt ("I have failed as a mother"). Additionally, she harbored a
secret fear that her son would become mentally ill, like her brother,
so whenever Aaron cried she worried it was the beginning of a mental breakdown. She tried to stave the breakdown off by coddling
Aaron. Mr. Bloom, who himself had had a passive and ineffectual
father, felt paralyzed by his son's behavior. When his son had trouble
falling asleep or getting up in the morning, Mr. Bloom cast about in
his own mind for ideas about what to do, and came up blank. So when
his wife yelled at him the way his own mother had yelled at his father,
it confirmed Mr. Bloom's sense of himself as stupid and weak.

With some work, the couple was able to see that these unresolved
issues from their own childhoods were contributing to their son's difficulties. Mrs. Bloom's inability to set limits on her son's behavior was
an unconscious reaction against her own parents' unavailability. Mr.
Bloom's inability to get involved with his wife and son reflected an
unconscious identification with his passive father.

Because we could see that Aaron's struggles were primarily the
result of their own inner conflicts, the Blooms agreed to work with
me in couple therapy rather than have me treat their son individually. Even though they felt bad when they realized they had contributed to his problems, they were relieved at having a way to think
about their family's troubles and work on them. When the couple
resolved their issues to the point that they were able to enforce a bedtime and morning routine for Aaron, his symptoms subsided.

If you see a child therapist for a consultation, she will make an
assessment about whether the difficulties originate in your family or

if they exist mainly in your child. The therapist will then recommend family or couple therapy, or individual therapy for your child. If the therapist is a good one, though, you should feel understood, supported, and relieved, regardless of the recommendation. If you feel the therapist is blaming you, it may be time for a second opinion.

2. Therapy is a crutch; I want my child to learn to handle his own problems.

If a crutch is something you lean on as you heal, then, yes, therapy is a good one. The point of therapy is not to foster dependence, but rather independence. Child therapists, like adult therapists, help their clients figure out why they are having difficulty managing and develop the skills to manage better. And the good news is that children, because they haven't lived as long and are not as fixed in their habits, learn much more quickly and easily than we do.

> **If a crutch is something you lean on as you heal, then, yes, therapy is a good one.**

3. My child will be stigmatized.

Some parents think that if they bring their child to therapy other people will think less of him, or he will think less of *himself*. Such a parent might say, "We can't bring Johnny to therapy. He'll think we think he's crazy." Newsflash: there is nothing more stigmatizing to a kid than suffering with anxiety or depression, because symptoms get in the way of normal social functioning. If your child is unhappy, the problem will show itself in her friendships and at school. Therapy is private, but emotional problems in kids are public knowledge, even if you wish nobody knew.

Children with emotional problems already feel there is something wrong with them. If you present therapy as something that will help them to feel better about themselves, they will usually be relieved that you know they need help and that you are willing to get it for them.

4. My child will outgrow the problem.

Well, maybe. Particularly if your child's struggles are a reaction to a specific event, such as a divorce or death, they may be normal and transitory. But in deciding whether your child's symptoms warrant a mental health consultation, use the criteria I outlined for you in Chapter One. The important question is whether your child's problems seem to be persisting for too long, or becoming *fixed*. If the answer is yes, it is time to get help. Remember, early intervention is the key. The sooner you seek help, the less time she's likely to be in therapy, and the less chance there is of her problem affecting her future development. For instance, if your child is unlucky enough to be physically or sexually assaulted (even fondled), the most important factor in determining how well your child recovers from the experience is the amount of support your family and trusted others provide. Frequently, immediate help from a therapist can lessen the impact of such a frightening event to the point that it becomes only a bad memory, not a bad turning point.

> **Early intervention is the key. The sooner you seek help, the less time your child is likely to be in therapy, and the less chance there is of her problem affecting her future development.**

5. My child refuses to go.

You don't consult your child about medical treatment. If the doctor prescribes an antibiotic, your kid has to take it, no matter how much he protests. Therapy should be no different. If you've decided it's important for your child to see a therapist, then yours should be the final word on the matter. You should prepare your child thoughtfully (more on that in a minute), but don't give him a choice. If he says "I'll go but you can't make me talk," say "fine." Let the therapist deal with his resistance. And don't, by any means, give your child decision-making power over the choice of therapist. You do the interviewing, and you choose the person you think is best. If that arrangement seems not to be working, a good therapist will help you decide what to do next.

PREPARING YOUR CHILD FOR THERAPY: THE FIVE KEY ELEMENTS

THE IDEA of child therapy is much more complicated and anxiety-producing for parents than for their children. Most of the children I see are relieved and happy to be there, and don't have any trouble understanding my role or the nature of our work together. Still, you may have anxiety about introducing the idea of therapy to your child, and you may encounter some resistance. What's the best way to break the news?

1. **Wait for a calm moment.** Don't raise the issue of therapy when either of you is angry or upset, especially following an argument or crisis (such as the child running away). If she's riled up, your daughter won't be able to take in what you're saying. And if you're angry, she's likely to think of therapy as a punishment.

2. **Identify the problem.** Tell your child what you see that has you worried for him. You might say, "Honey, I know you've been getting in a lot of fights at school." Or: "Daddy and I have noticed that you've been having a lot of nightmares lately."

3. **Offer compassion.** Tell your child you know he's been unhappy and you want to help. For example, say, "It must be really hard to have the other kids angry at you." Or: "Nightmares can be really scary. No one likes to be scared."

4. **Explain therapy.** Once you've identified the problem and offered compassion, tell your child you've been to see someone who can help. You might say something like: "Sometimes when children like you feel scared a lot of the time, it helps to go to a person whose job it is to help kids understand their feelings and

worries by talking and playing about them. Daddy and I went to meet a person like that last week. Her name is Dr. Kelly, and she's really nice. She's a kind of doctor for feelings, not for your body. We think if you met with her a few times, it might help you to understand better why you've been having all those nightmares. Then you wouldn't have to feel so scared."

5. **Don't get discouraged.** No matter how gentle you are, your child may become angry or defensive. He may say, "There's nothing wrong with me," or "I don't get nightmares anymore." Remain calm and stay the course. Just say, "OK, well, if you and the therapist decide that you aren't scared anymore, Daddy and I will be very happy. But we love you, and for now this is what we think best."

6. I want my child to talk to me, not to some stranger.

Some parents get a little jealous at the idea of their child opening up to a stranger, especially if communication hasn't been great at home. There are lots of reasons that it might be easier for your child to talk to a therapist than to you. The main reason is that you, and therefore your approval, are much more important to your child than the therapist is. Maybe your child is afraid of hurting you by seeming critical of you, of appearing too babyish with you, or of letting you down. Speaking to a therapist can be the first step in your child's being more open with you. Improving your child's ability to be close to you and to other key people is a primary goal of therapy.

> **Speaking to a therapist can be the first step in your child's being more open with you. Improving your child's ability to be close to you and to other key people is a primary goal of therapy.**

7. I don't want someone putting ideas into my child's head.

Children want, and need, to know *why* and *how*. Often, kids won't bring up certain subjects, or won't press them, if they've learned that these subjects make you uncomfortable. For example, if you offer the stork explanation when your child asks where babies come from, she won't really buy it (at least not for long), but she might not ask again. Instead, she'll have to rely on friends or figure out her own explanation. And whatever she comes up with will be wrong, and probably much scarier and more confusing than the truth. If your child is unhappy, he'll look for an explanation for that, too. And unless you give him a reason not to, he'll decide that he's the one responsible for everything that's going wrong. Coming to therapy doesn't put ideas in children's heads, it offers a realistic understanding of the ones that are already there.

8. Therapy will open up a Pandora's Box.

It might. But if this is a worry for you, that fact alone indicates that your child probably has a lot of scary thoughts and feelings buried away. Therapy *can* uncover hidden problems, or more serious problems than the ones you originally sought help for. But suppressed childhood difficulties don't go away by themselves. They linger and cause more serious problems down the road. The sooner you can help your child to face her troubling thoughts—whatever they are— the better.

> Therapy *can* uncover hidden problems, or more serious problems than the ones you originally sought help for. But suppressed childhood difficulties don't go away by themselves. They linger and cause more serious problems down the road.

9. My child doesn't have time.

Kids these days are incredibly busy, often too busy. Between school, homework, sports, clubs, and other activities, your child may have almost no free time. Taking piano lessons is important, but not crucial. There will be plenty of time later for the extras. If your daughter is unhappy or struggling, giving her therapy so she can develop a solid emotional foundation is much more important. Without it, none of the other stuff matters.

10. We can't afford it

Think of all the things you do for your child, even when money is tight. What about that vacation you didn't take so you could send her to camp, or that time you didn't go out to dinner for months so you could buy him a computer? Even though your child would strenuously disagree, nothing else you can buy him is as valuable as therapy, if he needs it. Also, there are several ways to get good, affordable help (see Chapter Seven).

What Is Play Therapy?

If you're a parent, you know that children rarely talk about their feelings directly until they are close to adolescence. Even if they say they're sad or mad, they can't go much beyond the general words. They certainly can't be expected to sit in a therapist's office and converse the way adults do. Children express their inner worlds by playing about them. Besides being fun, play gives kids a medium in which to work out their conflicts and explore new feelings and ways of being.

Child therapists are "play therapists." Like adult therapists, play therapists work first to establish a strong and trusting therapeutic relationship with their clients. A play therapist is likely to get down on the floor with your child and play with the materials in the office: a dollhouse, Play-Doh, puppets, or drawing materials. A play therapist is trained to understand the meaning of children's play, and to communicate that meaning back to them. The way the therapist does this will depend on the age and developmental stage of your child. Sometimes the therapist's comments will stay within the play. ("I think that teddy is really angry at his mommy for having another baby, look how he is throwing the little baby bear around.") At other times, the comments will be more direct. ("Gosh, that teddy is really being rough on its little brother. I bet you're feeling angry about the new baby in your family, too.")

Do Teenagers Play in Therapy?

Generally speaking, the older the child, the more talking there is and the less playing. By the time they're teenagers, most kids can reasonably be expected to sit in a chair for most or all of their session. But there are no hard and fast rules. Some adolescents, especially if they're emotionally guarded, are more able to talk about themselves if they can do it while they're playing a game, such as chess or cards. Others like to draw during sessions, and then talk about what they've created.

Will My Child's Therapist Report to Me on My Child's Progress?

Confidentiality is tricky when it comes to kids. On the one hand, children won't feel safe to open up in therapy unless they can be assured that what they say will be kept private. On the other hand, as a parent, you have a right to know how your child is getting along. In general, I tell children that while I'll be speaking to their parents from time to time, I won't share specifics of our work unless the child and I have agreed beforehand. The exception (and I make this explicit if I have any sense it may be an issue) is that if I ever have information that the child is suicidal or involved in any dangerous activities, I will have to inform the parents. But even in cases where I feel I must report something that a child has told me in confidence, I will inform the child and explore his feelings first.

Protecting your child's feeling of privacy and keeping you "in the loop" are not mutually exclusive. The younger your child, the more often the therapist should meet with you. These contacts will give you a chance to update the therapist about events in your child's life (the therapist will be interested in your information and opinions), and to voice any new concerns. At these meetings you're entitled to a general report about how your child is progressing. The therapist should also offer you guidance on managing your child better at home.

Where to Go for Help

Once you have decided to seek a consultation, you'll want to be sure to find the best person. After all, you'll be trusting her with the care of someone who means the world to you. Take your time, meet more than one therapist (two or three is best), and see them for several sessions, if need be, before deciding. You can use the same referral sources that I outlined in Chapter Seven. Here are a few questions you should consider as you go:

- Is this person a good listener who's taking the time to get to know me and my child?"
- Is this person warm and empathic?
- Is this person smart and experienced?
- Do I like and trust this person, and feel that I could work with her?
- Do I feel that my child will like and trust this person, too?

TIPS FOR HELPING YOUR CHILD SUCCEED IN THERAPY

■ Don't "grill" your child after sessions.

I know this is a tall order, but try to resist the urge to ask your child for reports on his therapy. Questions like "What did you and Dr. Kelly talk about today?" are likely to meet with either silence or an answer that's designed to please you. It's much better to let your child's therapy be a private place, and to use your meetings with his therapist to get the information you need.

■ **Remind your child that she has therapy as a resource, but don't harp on it.**

When issues or difficulties come up for your child, there's nothing wrong with gently suggesting that she talk about them in therapy. For example, if your daughter gets in a fight at school, you could say, "You know, honey, if you feel like talking with Dr. Kelly about what happened, she might be able to help you with the problems you're having on the playground." But try not to bring therapy up too often, or your child will feel you're intruding. If there's something you want your child's therapist to know, the best bet may be to call her yourself. It's best to inform your child beforehand, though, so he won't feel the adults are conspiring.

■ **Don't use therapy as a threat or form of discipline.**

A comment like "If you don't start cooperating I'm going to tell Dr. Kelly" is counterproductive. A better one would be: "Lately it's been really hard for you to cooperate with me and Daddy. I think it would be a good idea for us to talk to Dr. Kelly about ways we could help you manage better at home, so we can all get along better."

Beyond Therapy (and Back Again)

NOW THAT YOU'VE read this book, or at least the parts that answer *your* questions, you can decide if you want to give therapy a try. Maybe you feel excited and ready to jump right in. But maybe you feel timid or unsure. It'll be easier to face your fears if you remember that going into therapy really isn't like going on Dr. Phil's show. No matter who you are, what problems you have, or how worried you feel about starting, a good therapist won't shame you by confronting you with your faults or ordering you to change. If you take a little time to find the right match, you'll feel understood and supported—even when the going gets a little rough.

What will life be like afterward? Can we ever hope to be completely happy? No. Even when therapy goes well, it doesn't change who we fundamentally are. Our core personalities, and therefore our vulnerabilities, persist throughout our lives. If you're someone who panics about being left alone, therapy might help you to be less anxious about saying "good-bye." It might even help you enjoy some periods of time by yourself. But it's not going to turn you into a person who relishes solitude.

As we face new challenges in life, old issues can come up in new ways. For example, a woman who had an abusive father could be helped in therapy to trust another man enough to get married. But even if the marriage were happy, she might find that old feelings about her father resurfaced when she became pregnant or when her children approached the age at which she was abused. The woman would now have to integrate her old feelings about her father into her new role as a parent.

If you feel the need to return for more therapy, it doesn't mean that your past therapy was unsuccessful. Developmental challenges such as marriage, parenthood, the death of a parent, or having an older child leave home often prompt us to go back into treatment. These challenges can offer good opportunities to learn something new about ourselves or to grow in new ways. Some people return for a quick "touch-up," others to work on a bigger piece of unfinished business. It's normal, common, and often a good idea to revisit therapy many times over the course of our lives. And if you do return, you won't be starting over; you'll be building on an already good foundation. Therapy is often easier the second time around.

> **Developmental challenges such as marriage, parenthood, the death of a parent, or having an older child leave home often prompt us to go back into treatment. These challenges can offer good opportunities to learn something new about ourselves or to grow in new ways.**

Should you return to your old therapist? Sometimes you can't—he's died, retired, or moved away. But if you liked your therapist, thought you worked well with him, and *can* go back, there are obvious benefits. For one thing, he'll already know you, so you won't have to spend much time catching him up on your history. And you'll already have a relationship to draw on in working together, so you won't have to start from scratch. On the other hand, if you have mixed feelings about your old therapist or think someone new would force you to "stretch" in new ways, that's fine too. None of these decisions is cast in stone anyway, and you can always change your mind.

But all that is in the future. This is your life now. If you're suffering any kind of emotional pain, ask yourself: "Has this been going on too long? Do I really want to live this way?" Choosing therapy means choosing a better quality of life. You don't have to cope alone; help is a phone call away.

Resources

THE FOLLOWING ORGANIZATIONS offer information and referral services to the public:

PROFESSIONAL ORGANIZATIONS

Association for Autonomous Psychoanalytic Institutes (AAPI)
1800 Fairburn Avenue, #201
Los Angeles, CA 90025
www.aapionline.org

American Association for Marriage and Family Therapy (AAMFT)
112 South Alfred St.
Alexandria, VA 22314
703-838-9808
www.aamft.org

American Association of Pastoral Counselors (AAPC)
9504 Lee Highway
Fairfax, VA 22031
703-385-6967
www.aapc.org

American Association of Sex Educators, Counselors, and Therapists (AASECT)
PO Box 5488
Richmond, VA 23220
www.aasect.org

American Family Therapy Academy (AFTA)
1608 20th St., N.W.
Washington, DC 20009
202-483-8001
www.afta.org

American Group Psychotherapy Association (AGPA)
25 E. 21st St., 6th Floor
New York, NY 10010
212-477-2677
www.agpa.org

American Mental Health Counselors Association (AMHCA)
801 N. Fairfax St.
Suite 304
Alexandria, VA 22314
703-548-6002
800-326-2642
www.amhca.org

American Psychiatric Association (APA, not to be confused with the other APAs, the American *Psychoanalytic* Association and the American *Psychological* Association, see below)
1000 Wilson Blvd.
Suite 1825
Arlington, VA 22209
703-907-7300
www.psych.org

American Psychiatric Nurses Association (APNA)
1555 Wilson Blvd.
Suite 602
Arlington, VA 22209
703-243-2443
www.apna.org

American Psychoanalytic Association (APA)
309 E. 49th St.
New York, NY 10017
212-752-0450
www.apsa.org

American Psychological Association (APA)
750 1st St., N.E.
Washington, DC 20002
202-336-5500
www.apa.org

American Psychological Association Division of Psychoanalysis (Division 39) Section of Psychologist Psychoanalytic Practitioners (Section 1)
www.division39.org

Council of Psychoanalytic Psychotherapists (CPP)
www.cpp1.com

National Association for the Advancement of Psychoanalysis (NAAP)
80 Eighth Ave.
Suite 1501
New York, NY 10011
212-741-0515
www.naap.org

National Association of Social Workers (NASW)
750 1st St., N.E.
Suite 700
Washington, DC 20002
www.socialworkers.org

Clinical Social Work Federation
National Membership Committee on Psychoanalysis in Clinical Social Work
www.nmcop.org

SELF-HELP AND SOCIAL SERVICE ORGANIZATIONS
(arranged alphabetically by topic)

AGING

Alzheimer's Disease Education and Referral Center (ADEAR)
800-438-4380
www.alzheimers.org
- ADEAR is a public, U.S.-government-funded resource for information about Alzheimer's disease.

National Institute on Aging (NIA)
Building 31, Room 5C27
31 Center Dr., MSC 2292
Bethesda, MD 20892
301-496-1752
www.nia.nih.gov
- The NIA disseminates information about health and research advances in the field of aging.

ANXIETY

Anxiety Disorders Association of America (ADAA)
8730 Georgia Ave.
Silver Spring, MD 20910
240-485-1001
www.adaa.org

National Center for Post-Traumatic Stress
Disorder (NCPTSD)
www.ncptsd.org
- The NCPTSD is part of the Department
  of Veterans Affairs, and its mission is to
  advance the clinical care and social welfare of America's veterans through
  research, education, and training in the
  science, diagnosis, and treatment of
  PTSD and stress-related disorders. The
  Web site is an educational resource
  concerning PTSD and other enduring
  consequences of traumatic stress.

Posttraumatic Stress Disorder Alliance
PTSD Alliance Resource Center
877-507-PTSD
www.ptsdalliance.org
- The PTSD Alliance is a group of professional and advocacy organizations that
  have joined forces to provide educational resources to individuals diagnosed with PTSD and their loved ones,
  those at risk for developing PTSD, and
  medical, healthcare, and other frontline
  professionals.

DEPRESSION

Depression and Bipolar Support Alliance
(DBSA)
730 N. Franklin St., Suite 501
Chicago, IL 60610-7224
800-826-3632
www.dbsalliance.org
- This patient-directed organization fosters understanding about the impact
  and management of depression and
  bipolar illness by providing up-to-date,
  scientifically-based tools and information to the public.

DEVELOPMENTAL/LEARNING
DISABILITIES

The Attention Deficit Disorder
Association (ADDA)
PO Box 543
Pottstown, PA 19464
www.add.org
- The ADDA is a national nonprofit providing information, resources, and net-
  working to adults with ADHD and to
  professionals working with them.

Attention Deficit Information Network
(AD-IN)
58 Prince St.
Needham, MA 02492
www.addinfonetwork.org
- The Attention Deficit Information Network, Inc. is a nonprofit volunteer
  organization offering support and information to families of children with
  ADD, adults with ADD, and professionals through a network of chapters.

Autism Research Institute (ARI)
4182 Adams Avenue
San Diego, CA 92116
www.autism.com/ari/
- The ARI is a nonprofit organization primarily devoted to conducting research,
  and to disseminating the results of
  research, on the causes of autism and
  on methods of preventing, diagnosing,
  and treating autism and other severe
  behavioral disorders of childhood.

Autism Society of America (ASA)
800-8AUTISM
www.autism-society.org
- The ASA promotes lifelong access and
  opportunity for all individuals within the
  autism spectrum and their families to
  be fully participating, included members of their communities.

Center for the Study of Autism (CSA)
PO Box 4538
Salem, OR 97302
www.autism.org
- The CSA provides information about
  autism to parents and professionals,
  and conducts research on the efficacy
  of various therapeutic interventions.

Children and Adults with Attention-Deficit/Hyperactivity Disorder (CHADD)
8181 Professional Place, Suite 150
Landover, MD 20785
www.chadd.org
National Resource Center on AD/HD (a program of CHADD)
800-233-4050
www.help4adhd.org
- CHADD is a national nonprofit agency offering education, advocacy, and support for individuals and families dealing with AD/HD.

Learning Disability Association of America (LDA)
4156 Library Rd.
Pittsburg, PA 15234-1349
412-341-1515
www.ldanatl.org
- This nonprofit volunteer organization advocates for individuals with learning disabilities and their families, through a network of local affiliates.

DOMESTIC VIOLENCE/SEXUAL ABUSE

Childhelp USA
15757 North 78th St.
Scottsdale, AZ 85260
800-4-A-CHILD
www.childhelpusa.org
- Childhelp USA is dedicated to meeting the physical, emotional, educational, and spiritual needs of abused and neglected children by focusing its efforts and resources in the areas of treatment, prevention, and research. Its programs and services include the operation of the Childhelp USA National Child Abuse Hotline.

National Clearinghouse on Child Abuse and Neglect Information
330 C Street SW
Washington, DC 20447
703-385-7565
800-FYI-3366
http://nccanch.acf.hhs.gov
- The National Clearinghouse on Child Abuse and Neglect Information, a service of the Children's Bureau, helps professionals locate information on child abuse and neglect and related child welfare issues.

National Domestic Abuse Hotline
800-799-SAFE

Rape, Abuse and Incest National Network (RAINN)
635-B Pennsylvania Ave., SE
Washington, DC 20003
202-544-1034
National Sexual Assault Hotline: 800-656-HOPE, extension one
www.rainn.org
- RAINN carries out programs to prevent sexual assault, help victims, and ensure that rapists are brought to justice. Among the services they offer is counseling resource information.

Safer Society Foundation, Inc.
PO Box 340
Brandon , VT 05733-0340
802-247-3132
www.safersociety.org
- The Safer Society Foundation, Inc., a nonprofit agency, is a national research, advocacy, and referral center for the prevention and treatment of sexual abuse.

Stop It Now!
PO Box 495
Haydenville, MA 01039
413-268-3096
1-888-PREVENT
info@stopitnow.org
www.stopitnow.org
- Stop it Now! is a national nonprofit working to prevent and ultimately eradicate child sexual abuse.

Survivors of Incest Anonymous
World Service Office
PO Box 190
Benson, MD 21018-9998
www.siawso.org

EATING DISORDERS

National Eating Disorders Association
(NEDA)
603 Steward St., Suite 803
Seattle, WA 98101
206-382-3587
www.nationaleatingdisorders.org
- NEDA is a nonprofit organization providing treatment referrals to those suffering from anorexia, bulimia, or binge
  eating disorder and those concerned
  with body image and weight issues.

Overeaters Anonymous (O.A.)
PO Box 44020
Rio Rancho, New Mexico 87124-4020
505-891-2664
www.overeatersanonymous.org

FINANCIAL/GAMBLING ISSUES

Debtors Anonymous (D.A.)
PO Box 920888
Needham, MA 02492-0009
781-453-2743
www.debtorsanonymous.org

Gamblers Anonymous (G.A.)
PO Box 17173
Los Angeles, CA 90017
213-386-8789
www.gamblersanonymous.org

National Council on Problem Gambling,
Inc. (NCPG)
208 G St., NE
Washington, DC 20002
202-547-9204
24-hour national hotline: 800-522-4700
www.ncpgambling.org
- The NCPG aims to increase public
  awareness of pathological gambling,
  ensure the widespread availability of
  treatment for problem gamblers and
  their families, and to encourage
  research and programs for prevention
  and education.

MENTAL HEALTH/MENTAL ILLNESS

National Alliance for the Mentally Ill
Colonial Place Three
2107 Wilson Blvd., Suite 300
Arlington, VA 22201-3042
703-524-7600
Member services: 800-950-NAMI
www.nami.org
- NAMI is a nonprofit, grassroots self-
  help, support, and advocacy organization of the mentally ill and the families
  and friends of people with severe mental illnesses, such as schizophrenia,
  schizoaffective disorder, bipolar disorder, major depressive disorder, obsessive-compulsive disorder, panic and
  other severe anxiety disorders, autism
  and pervasive developmental disorders,
  attention deficit/hyperactivity disorder,
  and other severe and persistent mental
  illnesses that affect the brain.

National Mental Health Services
Knowledge Exchange Network (KEN)
800-789-2647
- KEN is a service of the Center for Mental Health Services, and is a national
  clearinghouse providing information
  about federal, state, and local mental
  health service programs and advocacy
  organizations.

National Institute of Mental Health
(NIMH)
6001 Executive Blvd.
Room 8184, MSC 9663
Bethesda, MD 20892-9663
301-443-4513
www.nimh.nih.gov

SAMHSA's Mental Health Information
Center
PO Box 42557
Washington, DC 20015
800-789-2647
www.mentalhealth.org
- The Substance Abuse and Mental
  Health Services Administration's
  (SAMHSA) National Mental Health
  Information Center provides informa-
  tion about mental health via a toll-free
  number, its Web site, and more than
  six hundred publications.

SEXUAL DISTURBANCES

Sex Addicts Anonymous (SAA)
ISO SAA
PO Box 70949
Houston, TX 77270
713-869-4902
800-477-8191
www.sexaa.org

Sexaholics Anonymous (S.A.)
PO Box 3565
Brentwood, TN 37024
615-370-0882
www.sa.org

Sex and Love Addicts Anonymous
Fellowship-Wide Services
PO Box 338
Norwood, MA 02062-0338
www.slaafws.org

SUBSTANCE ABUSE

Alcoholics Anonymous (A.A.)
A.A. World Services, Inc.
Box 459 Grand Central Station
New York, NY 10163
212-870-3400
www.aa.org

American Council for Drug Education
800-488-DRUG
acde.org
■ The American Council for Drug Education is a substance abuse prevention and education agency that develops programs and materials based on the most current scientific research on drug use and its impact on society. ACDE offers a range of educational programs and services.

Cocaine Anonymous (C.A.)
www.ca.org (local listings available on the Web site)

Narcotics Anonymous (N.A.)
World Service Office
PO Box 9999
Van Nuys, CA 91409
818-773-9999
www.na.org

National Council on Alcoholism and Drug Dependence (NCADD)
20 Exchange Place, Suite 2902
New York, NY 10005
212-269-7797
HOPE LINE: 800/NCA-CALL (24-hour affiliate referral)
www.ncadd.org
■ NCADD provides education and information, and advocates prevention, intervention, and treatment through offices in New York and Washington, and a nationwide network of affiliates.

References

American Counseling Association Code of Ethics and Standards of Practice, 1995: www.counseling.org.

American Psychiatric Association Ethics Primer, 2001: www.psych.org/edu/res_fellows/ethicsprimer.cfm.

American Psychological Association Mental Health Patients Bill of Rights: Principles for the Provision of Mental Health and Substance Abuse Treatment Services, 1997: www.apa.org/pubinfo/rights/Rights.html.

———. *Ethical Principles of Psychology and Code of Conduct*, 2003: www.apa.org/ethics/.

*American Psychiatric Nurses Association Vision, Mission, and Principles:*www.apna.org/aboutapna/mission.html.

Beck, Judith S. *Cognitive Therapy*. New York: Guilford, 1995.

Berne, Eric. *Games People Play: The Basic Handbook of Transactional Analysis*. New York: Ballantine, 1996.

Blanck, Gertrude and Rubin Blanck. *Ego Psychology*. New York: Columbia University Press, 1992.

Bond, Frank and Windy Dryden, eds.. *Handbook of Brief Cognitive Behavior Therapy*. New York: John Wiley and Sons, 2002.

Chambless, D. L. and T. H. Ollendick. "Empirically Supported Psychological Interventions: Controversies and Practice." *Annual Review of Psychology* 52 (2001): 685–716.

Diagnostic and Statistical Manual of Mental Disorders DSM-IV-TR, 4th ed. Washington, D.C.: American Psychiatric Association, 2000.

Dobson, Keith, ed. *Handbook of Cognitive-Behavioral Therapies*, 2nd ed. New York: Guilford, 2002.

Dryden, Windy, Raymond DiGiuseppe, and Michael Neenan. *A Primer on Rational-Emotive Therapy*, 2nd ed. Champaign, IL: Research Press, 2002.

Engler, Jack, Ph.D. and Daniel Goleman, Ph.D. *The Consumer's Guide to Psychotherapy*. New York: Simon and Schuster, 1992.

Goman, Jack M. *The Essential Guide to Psychiatric Drugs*. New York: St. Martin's Press, 1995.

Gray, Anne. *An Introduction to the Therapeutic Frame*. New York: Routledge, 2000.

Hogan, Kevin and Kathy Hume, eds. *The New Hypnotherapy Handbook: Hypnosis and Mind/Body Healing,* 2nd revision. Minnesota: Network 3000, 2001.

International Coach Federation: The Nature and Scope of Coaching, 2004: www.coachfederation.org/aboutcoaching/nature.asp.

Koocher, G. P. and P. Keith-Spiegel. *Ethics in Psychology: Professional Standards and Cases,* 2nd ed. New York: Oxford University Press, 1998.

Kramer, Peter D. *Listening to Prozac*. New York: Penguin Books, 1997.

Levine, Ellen G. and Stephen K. Levine, eds. *Foundations of Expressive Arts Therapy: Theoretical and Clinical Perspective*. London: Jessica Kingsley, 1999.

McWilliams, Nancy. *Psychoanalytic Psychotherapy: A Practitioner's Guide*. New York: Guilford Press, 2004.

"Mental Health: Does Therapy Help?" *Consumer Reports,* November 1995.

Morrison, James, M.D. *Straight Talk About Your Mental Health*. New York: Guilford Press, 2002.

The National Association of Cognitive-Behavioral Therapists Online Headquarters: Cognitive-Behavioral Therapy: www.nacbt.org.

Perls, Fritz. *The Gestalt Approach and Eye Witness to Therapy*. Palo Alto, CA: Science and Behavior Books, 1973.

Polster, Erving and Miriam Polster. *Gestalt Therapy Integrated: Contours of Theory and Practice*. New York: Random House, 1974.

Scharff, Jill S. and David E. Scharff. *The Primer of Object Relations Therapy*. New York: Jason Aronson, 1995.

Schwartz, Mark and Frank Andrasik, eds. *Biofeedback: A Practitioner's Guide,* 3rd ed. New York: Guilford, 2003.

Seligman, M. E. P. "The Effectiveness of Psychotherapy: the Consumer Reports Study." *American Psychologist* 50, no. 12 (December 1995): 965–74.

Shapiro, Francis. *Eye Movement Desensitization and Reprocessing (EMDR), Basic Principles, Protocols, and Procedures,* 2nd ed. New York: Guilford, 2001.

Stein, Murray, ed. *Jungian Analysis (The Reality of the Psyche Series),* 2nd ed. Chicago: Open Court Press, 1995.

United States Association for Body Psychotherapy. "A Brief Description of Body Psychotherapy": www.usabp.org/displaycommon.cfm?an=1 &subarticlenbr=30.

Westen, Drew, Kate Morrison, and Heather Thompson-Brenner. "The Empirical Status of Empirically Supported Psychotherapies: Assumptions, Findings, and Reporting in Controlled Clinical Trials," *Psychological Bulletin*, 2004, Vol. 130, No.4, 631–663.

Wilbur, Ken. *Integral Psychology: Consciousness, Spirit, Psychology, Therapy*. Boston: Shambhala Publications, 2000.

Wilen, Timothy E. *Straight Talk About Psychiatric Medication for Kids*. New York: Guilford Press, 2002.

Winnicott, D. W. *Maturational Processes and the Facilitating Environment: Studies in the Theory of Emotional Development*, Reprinted Edition. London: Stylus Pub. Llc., 1996

Winnicott, D. W. *Playing and Reality*. London: Tavistock Publications, 1971.

White, Marjorie Taggart and Marcella Bakur Weiner. *The Theory and Practice of Self Psychology*. New York: Brunner/Mazel, 1986.

Yalom, Irvin D. *Existential Psychotherapy*. New York: Basic Books, 1980.

Yalom, Irvin D. *The Gift of Therapy: An Open Letter to a New Generation of Therapists and Their Patients*. New York: HarperCollins, 2002.

Young, Courtenay. "Body Psychotherapy: It's [sic] History and Present Day Scope." An address to the European Association for Body Psychotherapy, Rome, 1997: www.usabp.org/displaycommon.cfm?an=1 &subarticlenbr=11.

Acknowledgments

AS A THERAPIST you're always a student. I'm fortunate to have wise and generous teachers in my colleagues at my professional home, The International Psychotherapy Institute (formerly IIORT). Through their skill and openness, they facilitate my ongoing personal and professional growth, show me how far I still have to go, and inspire me to keep learning.

In this project, as in the rest of my life, I've relied on many good friends. I particularly want to acknowledge Mona Mendelson and Jan Dommerholt—who offer emotional and practical support to me and my family in all the ways and at all the times we need it. I value our friendship beyond words. I'm indebted also to Victoria Ruttenberg, professional coach extraordinaire, who helped me get out of my own way, and to Nancy Lasater, who gave my manuscript a generous helping of her time and attention. There's evidence of her wise advice throughout.

From my mother, Isabel Scharff, I'm still learning, every day, important lessons about important relationships. I'm not always a quick study, but my life and work are enhanced by her loving insights. My father, David Scharff, and stepmother, Jill Scharff, have encouraged and guided me always. They've mentored each phase of my career, and given me wonderful opportunities and gentle nudges when I needed them. My father read this book at several stages, and his thoughtful input was invaluable. I'm grateful to all three for the privilege of growing up understood, and for my own psychological-mindedness. My terrific half-sibs, Zoe, Xanthe, and Daniel Scharff, cheerfully distracted my kids so I could write, and have earned my thanks and their niece's and nephew's adoration. And Nell, my sister and best friend—this book was her idea, like most of the good things I do. She keeps me on track.

The multitalented Cara Barbierri managed to fit the job of research assistant and beloved babysitter into her busy study schedule. She'll be a great psychologist, but things in my household won't run as smoothly without her. My children, Chloe and Ben, have had to put up with my absences and preoccupations. They're my most important teachers.

Matthew Lore, my wonderful editor at Marlowe and Company, *got it* from the beginning. He took a chance on a first-timer, and gave me independence and guidance in perfect measure. His keen eye, discerning ear, and open mind made our collaboration a pleasure. Matthew's assistant, Peter Jacoby, facilitated every step of the process. He answered my questions, indulged my requests, and tolerated my obsessionality with competence and good humor.

Thanks to Ron Goldfarb for connecting me with my friend and agent, the incomparable Farley Chase. Without Farley's conceptual acumen, tenacity, and wry humor this book would not be. He'd have made a good therapist, but it was lucky for me he went another way.

And, finally, I owe a debt of gratitude to the patients I've worked with over the past seventeen years, in New York and Washington, D.C. Their trust, dedication, and spirit have enriched my life, and infuse the pages of this book.

Index

setting, for children, 154
between therapy and outside life, 88
treating friends of clients, 88, 116, 126–27
violation of professional, by therapist, 113
breathing techniques, 53, 54

C

cancellation policy of therapist, 125–26
career counselors, 44
caring in therapeutic relationships, 62, 68
categories of therapists. *See also* specialized
technique/s; theoretical orientation
modality/modalities, 11, 30, 46–51, 57
professional degree, 30, 40–43, 56–57
specialized interest/s, 31, 55–56, 57
chair or couch for therapy, 127–28
change
from dealing with painful feelings, 35
difficulty of accomplishing, xv–xvi, 72
long-term, vs. short-term symptom relief,
24
of negative behaviors, xiv–xv
one person changes, everyone feels it, 9
unconsciously working against, 63
characteristics of a good candidate for
therapy, 7
charismatic vs. warm therapists, 105
child custody issues, finding a therapist for,
55–57
children
alcoholic parents and, 18, 66–67
appropriate development of, 143–46
coping mechanisms, 64
depression or suicidality, 148
development stages, 143–46
diagnostic testing, 150
emotional problems are public knowledge,
155–56
gifts from therapist to, 126
infants, problems with, 148–49
parent's depression and, 8–9
routine, importance of, 59–60
sexually-assaulted, 156
therapist's right to share information with
parents of, 115, 161–62
child self vs. grown-up self, 64
child therapy
assessing where difficulties originate, 154–55
confidentiality, 161–62
finding a therapist, 157, 162
overview, 142–43
play therapy, 160–61
preparing your child for, 157–58
psychiatrists, training of, 41
reasons for, 48, 146–47

reasons for avoiding, 152, 155–60
choosing a therapist, 130. *See also* initial
consultation; shopping for a therapist;
entries beginning with questions
chronic pain, 53, 54, 55–57
client's goals, honoring, 22–23
clinical social workers, training of, 43
clinics, 90–92, 97
code of ethics. *See* ethics
cognitive/behavioral therapy
dialectical behavior therapy, 53–54
indications for treatment with, 34
initial interview, 101
psychodynamic therapy compared to,
35–37
reading list, 37–38
relationship of client and therapist, 36
sex therapy, 52–53
systematic desensitization, 33–34
cognitive capacities of preschool children, 145
cognitive therapy, 33, 34. *See also*
cognitive/behavioral therapy
college clinics, 90
community mental health clinics, 90–91
complaining, moving past, 20
complaints about therapist, filing, 120, 129
complementary modalities, 11
conditioning, cultural, 33. *See also*
cognitive/behavioral therapy
confidentiality
child therapy and parents, 161–62
ethics and, 114–15
exceptions to rules, 115
friends and, 21
insurance and, 24, 79, 115, 129
Patient's Bill of Rights, 129–30
rules of, for professionals, 114
consistent, not rigid, therapists, 105–6
consultation appointment. *See* initial
consultation
contractual limitations affecting treatment,
129
coping with unchangeable situations, 10, 63
core beliefs and values, 37
core personalities, 165
cost considerations
affordability of therapy, 13–14, 160
insurance and, 78–81
therapy bargains, 92–95
couch or chair for therapy, 127–28
couple therapy, 47, 81–82, 153–54. *See also*
reasons for avoiding therapy; reasons for
seeking therapy
credentialing board, 116, 120
crisis, psychodynamic therapy and, 32
criticism from therapists, 137

predetermined ideas as block to progress, 4
preparing to leave therapy, 140
preschool stage, 145
"Principles for the Provision of Mental Health and Substance Abuse Treatment Services" (American Psychological Association), 114
private practice, 97–100
problematic behaviors as reasons for seeking therapy, 3
problems
    containing, for entire family, 47
    defining personal, 77
    diffuse nature of, 4
    indicating need for help (in list form), 5–6
    value of talking about, 16–19
procedure codes, 80, 115
professional counselors, licensed, 43
professional degree therapists, 30, 40–43, 56–57
professional organizations, list of, 131–32, 168–69
psychiatric medications reading list, 51. *See also* medication therapy
psychiatric nurses, training of, 43
psychiatric terminology, 22, 29
psychiatrists, 41–42. *See also* medication therapy
psychoanalysis training programs as source for therapy, 92–95
psychoanalysts, 45–46
psychoanalytic therapy, 49. *See also* psychodynamic therapy
psychodynamic therapy
    basics, list of, 72
    cognitive/behavioral therapy compared to, 35–37
    free association, 64–68
    initial interview, 101
    interpretations, 70–71
    long-term or short-term therapy, 33, 83–84
    overview, 31–32, 62–64
    reading list, 38
    relationship of client and therapist, 36
    secrets, talking about, 67–68
    transference, 68–69
    treatment method indications, 32
    working through, 71–72
psychological aspects of a problem, identifying, 11
psychological effects of physical pain, finding a therapist for, 55–57
psychological factors of ADHD, 151
psychologists, 42, 44, 150
psychopharmacologists, 42

psychotherapy, 58, 89–90
psychotic disorders, finding a therapist for, 55–57

Q

qualities common to all good therapies, 58–62
qualities to look for in a therapist, 104–8
questions to ask a clinic, 97
questions to ask a therapist. *See also* fees
    cancellation policy, 125–26
    emergency coverage policy, 126
    during initial consultation, 109
    during initial phone call, 98–99
    schedule flexibility, 15, 84
    technique-related, 56–57
    vacation policy, 125
questions to ask yourself
    after initial consultation, 109
    demographics of therapist, 82–83
    insurance and cost considerations, 78–81
    list of, xvi
    logistics issues, 84
    long-term or short-term preference, 83–84
    problems (determining what to deal with), 77
    psychiatric medications, interest in, 82
    schedule considerations, 15, 84
    training of therapist (*See* theoretical orientation)
    type of therapy (individual, couple, family, group), 81–82

R

rage, example of, 17–19
rational/emotive therapy reading list, 38
reasons for avoiding therapy
    for children, 152, 155–60
    cost, 13–14, 160
    fear of never being done with, 21
    no one is smart enough to help me, 104–5
    painful memories create resistance, 135–37
    self-indulgence and whining associated with, 19–20
    stigma from, 23–24
    talking will make problems worse, 16–19
    talking with stranger won't help, 20–21
    therapist will want to fix everything, 22–23
    therapy doesn't work, 24–25
    therapy is for crazy people, 22
    time, 14–16
    you're convinced problem lies outside you, 10